WHO MAKES YOUR TEEN HEART BEAT?

Tom Cruise? Rob Lowe? Lisa Bonet? Don't you want to know how to get in touch with Kirk Cameron . . . Bon Jovi . . . Ally Sheedy? Thumb through this star-studded directory and find out, firsthand, the real story of how they all got started. Learn what drives them, what they do for fun. You'll love the inside information you pick up about today's young TV, movie and rock celebrities. The hip, the handsome, the sultry and the sensitive — they're all here. So take a good long look before you sign off on

THE TEEN STAR YEARBOOK

GRACE CATALANO

TEEN STAR YEARBOOK

PaperJacks LTD.

TORONTO   NEW YORK

AN ORIGINAL

PaperJacks

TEEN STAR
YEARBOOK

PaperJacks LTD.

300 STEELCASE RD. E., MARKHAM, ONT. L3R 2M1
210 FIFTH AVE., NEW YORK, N.Y. 10010

First edition published July 1988

10 9 8 7 6 5 4 3 2

ISBN 0-7701-0937-3

PHOTO ACKNOWLEDGEMENTS

John Paschal/Celebrity Photo, Steve Granitz/Celebrity Photo, Capital Cities/ABC, Inc., Karen Hardy/LGI, Dave Hogan/LGI, Frank Edwards/Pictorial Parade, Darlene Hammond/Pictorial Parade, Andy Freeberg/Retna, Paul Rider/Retna, Gary Gershoff/Retna, Robin Platzer/Images, Ryder Public Relations, Bob Gruen/Star File, Janet Macoska/Star File, Chuck Pulin/Star File, Todd Kaplan/Star File, Vinnie Zuffante/Star File, Ken Katz/Star File, Kate Simon/Star File, Paul Natkin/Star File

TELEVISION STARS

Alf
Chad Allen
Mackenzie Astin (John Paschal/Celebrity Photo)
Scott Baio (Vinnie Zuffante/Star File)
Jason Bateman (Steve Granitz/Celebrity Photo)
Justine Bateman (Vinnie Zuffante/Star File)
Brian Bloom
Lisa Bonet (Vinnie Zuffante/Star File)
Kirk Cameron (Capital Cities/ABC, Inc.)
Johnny Depp
Andrea Elson
Michael J. Fox (Karen Hardy/LGI)
Tracey Gold (Capital Cities/ABC, Inc.)
Benji Gregory
Scott Grimes (Courtesy Ryder Public Relations)
Nancy McKeon (Frank Edwards/Pictorial Parade)
Alyssa Milano (Courtesy Ryder Public Relations)
Jeremy Miller (Capital Cities/ABC, Inc.)
Michael Pare
Pat Petersen (Courtesy Ryder Public Relations)
Brian Robbins (Capital Cities/ABC, Inc.)
Ricky Schroder (Darlene Hammond/Pictorial Parade)
John Stamos (Robin Platzer/Images)
Scott Valentine (Courtesy Ryder Public Relations)
Malcolm-Jamal Warner (Todd Kaplan/Star File)
Jonathan Ward
Tina Yothers (Vinnie Zuffante/Star File)

MOVIE STARS

Sean Astin (John Paschal/Celebrity Photo)
Kevin Bacon (Ken Katz/Star File)
Matthew Broderick (Vinnie Zuffante/Star File)
Tom Cruise (Vinnie Zuffante/Star File)
Jon Cryer

Matt Dillon (Kate Simon/Star File)
Emilio Estevez
Corey Feldman (Vinnie Zuffante/Star File)
Andre Gower
Corey Haim (Courtesy Ryder Public Relations)
C. Thomas Howell (Vinnie Zuffante/Star File)
Ryan Lambert
Rob Lowe (Paul Natkin/Star File)
Andrew McCarthy (Robin Platzer/Images)
Ralph Macchio (Vinnie Zuffante/Star File)
Lou Diamond Phillips
River Phoenix (Vinnie Zuffante/Star File)
Molly Ringwald (Vinnie Zuffante/Star File)
Ally Sheedy
Charlie Sheen
Eric Stoltz (Frank Edwards/Pictorial Parade)
Wil Wheaton

ROCK STARS

A-HA
Mags Furuholem (Paul Rider/Retna)
Morten Harket (Dave Hogan/LGI)
Pal Waaktaar (Paul Rider/Retna)

BON JOVI
Jon Bon Jovi
David Bryan
Richie Sambora
Alec John Such
Tico Torres

DURAN DURAN
Simon Le Bon (Chuck Pulin/Star File)
Nick Rhodes (Retna)
John Taylor (Robin Platzer/Images)

Corey Hart (Gary Gershoff/Retna)
Whitney Houston (Todd Kaplan/Star File)
Billy Idol (Andy Freeberg/Retna)
Michael Jackson (Vinnie Zuffante/Star File)
Joan Jett (Todd Kaplan/Star File)
Cyndi Lauper (Todd Kaplan/Star File)
Julian Lennon (Bob Gruen/Star File)
Madonna (Vinnie Zuffante/Star File)

MENUDO
Ray Acevedo
Ruben Gomez (Chuck Pulin/Star File)
Sergio Gonzales
Ricky Martin
Ralphy Rodriguez

George Michael

THE NEW MONKEES (Robin Platzer/Images)
Jared Chandler
Dino Kovas
Marty Ross
Larry Saltis

Jack Wagner (Capital Cities/ABC, Inc.)
Paul Young (Janet Macoska/Star File)
Dweezil Zappa (Darlene Hammond/Pictorial Parade)

For Ralph and Grace, with love

Table of Contents

Part One — Television Stars

Part Two — Movie Stars

Part Three — Rock Stars

A-HA

BON JOVI

DURAN DURAN

PART ONE
TELEVISION STARS

ALF

He is furry, 229 years old, three feet high and hilarious. His name is Alf (which stands for Alien Life Form) and he stars in his own TV series.

He was born Gordon Shumway to three parents and grew up on the planet Melmac. A graduate of Melmac High School, Alf was a champion Spleen player. What's Spleen? "I will have to show you sometime," he says. "It's a complicated game with a baseball glove and a fork."

Alf says life on Melmac was different from life on Earth. For example, his favorite food is cats and his height fluctuates with his weight. Astrology on Melmac was also quite different. "We had two signs," he says. "Sagittarius and non-Sagittarius. I'm Sagittarius."

Before he crashed into the roof of the Tanner family's garage, Alf worked a dozen years as an orbit guard on his planet. The show business bug bit him when he was around 123 years old and he worked as a part-time male model back on Melmac. "Yeah, I did some modeling," he says. "But what I *really* wanted to do was direct."

Unfortunately, Alf's planet exploded. "Everyone got off it," he notes. "They are all still scattered up there." Fortunately for us, Alf's spaceship crashed right into the funniest sitcom on television.

The cast of his show are one big, happy family and, he says, smiling, "They are a nice group of people, but they need my help once in a while." Alf loves being a star on Earth and getting a chance to star in his own TV series, a Saturday morning cartoon about his adventures on Melmac and an upcoming feature film. He is so popular that toy stores carry an Alf doll. When he was asked to comment on that, he replied nonchalantly, "No problem! Imitation is the sincerest form of flattery!"

ALF'S VITAL STATISTICS

FULL REAL NAME: ALF (Alien Life Form)

BIRTHDATE/AGE: August 12 and October 2. He's 229 years old.

BIRTHPLACE: The planet Melmac — Lower East Side

HEIGHT/WEIGHT: About three feet — fluctuates with weight

HAIR: Burnt Sienna

EYES: Off-black

SIGN: "On Melmac, we have two signs, Sagittarius and non-Sagittarius. I'm Sagittarius."

FAMILY: Three parents, still living.

EDUCATION: Melmac High School — 122 years; College — Melmac State 2 years. Majored in PED-ED which stands for Pedestrian Crossing, of course!

EARLY JOB: "I was a part-time male model on Melmac."

CURRENT RESIDENCE: Burbank, California, currently at the Oakwood.

MARITAL STATUS: Single. "I'm looking for a woman with more hair than I've got. Someone suggested Charo."

FAVORITE FOOD: Cats

FAVORITE PASTIME: "I used to collect barbed wire and go out dancing a lot."

FAVORITE QUOTE: "I've got dandruff older than your country!"

FONDEST MEMORY OF MELMAC: "It was sort of like living in Rhode Island. It's a small planet and that's about it."

THOUGHTS ABOUT EARTH: "On Melmac, the sky was green and the grass blue, so I feel like I'm living upside down."

WHERE TO WRITE TO ALF: Alf
c/o NBC-TV
3000 West Alameda Avenue
Burbank, CA 91523

CHAD ALLEN

The Witherspoons of *Our House* are a close and loving TV family. As David Witherspoon, Chad Allen loves being part of that family and plays his role superbly.

He was born Chad Allen Lazzari on June 5, 1974 and credits his parents, Ed and Faith, for giving him the encouragement he needed as a young actor. He began doing commercials at age seven and has appeared on TV in *Webster* and in a recurring role as Dr. Westphall's autistic son on *St. Elsewhere*.

When he auditioned for *Our House*, he had to go to school in the afternoon. "I waited to hear if I got the part, but no one called," he says. His father eventually answered the call which brought the good news that Chad had been cast. "There was a lot of excitement around my house that night," he remembers.

When this cute, blond-haired actor has spare time, he enjoys reading mystery and adventure stories, making jewelry out of rocks and playing basketball. He is close to his three older brothers, Steven, Bobby and Jimmy and twin sister, Charity, and loves taking care of his pet turtle, O.J.

He says his TV character is different from his own personality, but there are a few similarities. "We're both a little headstrong at times and try to be better than we are," he says.

Thinking ahead to his future, Chad would like to continue acting. A fan of actor Robert Redford, he wants to star in an adventure film and dreams of becoming a director. As for his personal ambition, Chad reflects, "I'd like to have a ranch in Utah and a wife and family."

CHAD ALLEN'S VITAL STATISTICS

FULL REAL NAME: Chad Allen Lazzari

BIRTHDATE: June 5, 1974

BIRTHPLACE: Cerritos, California

HAIR: Blond

EYES: Blue/green

HEIGHT: 5′

WEIGHT: 85 lbs.

FAMILY: Dad, Ed; mom, Faith; twin sister, Charity; older brothers, Steven, Bobby, Jimmy

TV ROLE: David Witherspoon on *Our House*

TV SHOWS: *St. Elsewhere*, *Simon and Simon*, *Webster*

MOVIES: Chad filmed an upcoming feature film, *Terrorvision*, in Rome, Italy

HOBBIES: Fishing, making jewelry out of rocks

PETS: One turtle named O.J., two crabs

FAVORITE SPORTS: Basketball, swimming, skateboarding

FAVORITE COLOR: Green

FAVORITE SUBJECT IN SCHOOL: Science (he's in the 8th grade)

FAVORITE ACTORS: Jason Robards, Robert Redford

FAVORITE FOOD: "Mom's homemade spaghetti and pizza!"

WHAT CHAD LOOKS FOR IN A GIRL: "Honesty and truthfulness!"

IDEA OF A FUN DATE: "The movies and dinner in a quiet restaurant."

BEST QUALITY: "I try to be honest with myself and other people."

FAVORITE QUOTE: "What you are is God's gift to you. What you become is your gift to God."

FUTURE GOALS: "I'd like to be acting in adventure films and directing. I'd like to have a ranch in Utah and a wife and family."

WHERE TO WRITE TO CHAD: Chad Allen
c/o NBC-TV
3000 West Alameda Avenue
Burbank, CA 91523

MACKENZIE ASTIN

Mackenzie Astin, who plays Andrew Moffat in *The Facts of Life*, hadn't originally planned on becoming an actor. It was after he saw his brother Sean in *Please Don't Hit Me Mom* with their mother, Patty Duke, that Mackenzie knew he wanted to be an actor, too. "Sean was eight and I was six," he says. "Up until that time all I wanted to do was play baseball, but suddenly everything changed."

The youngest son of actress Patty Duke and actor John Astin, Mackenzie first drew attention when he played the Nelsons' son, TJ, in the TV movie *I Dream of Jeannie: 15 Years Later*. He guest-starred on an episode of *Hotel* and then received the good news that he'd won his role on *The Facts of Life*.

When he started on the show, he was only in a couple of episodes. But more lines were quickly written for him. "In the beginning, I was in school more than I was in the studio," recalls Mackenzie, who admits that being an actor has its advantages and disadvantages. He is quick to point out how his life has changed because he is on TV each week.

"It's awkward when I meet new friends," he says. "Sometimes someone will like me and want to be my friend just because I'm on *Facts of Life* and I don't like that at all."

Mackenzie made his feature film debut in *The Garbage Pail Kids'* movie and says the experience was great! "I definitely want to do more films." He confides that his dream is to play a pirate in a big screen adventure and says he looks forward to a long career as an actor.

When Mackenzie has some time off, he likes going to the movies or hanging out with his friends in Los Angeles' hip Westwood Village.

MACKENZIE ASTIN'S VITAL STATISTICS

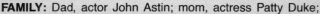

FULL REAL NAME: Mackenzie Alexander Astin

NICKNAMES: Skeezix, Mack, Mackie

BIRTHDATE: May 12, 1973

BIRTHPLACE: Los Angeles, California

HEIGHT: 5'1"

WEIGHT: 90 lbs.

HAIR: Sandy blond

EYES: Blue/green

FAMILY: Dad, actor John Astin; mom, actress Patty Duke; brother Sean; half-brothers Al, Dave, Tom

TV ROLE: Andrew Moffat on *The Facts of Life*

TV MOVIE: *I Dream of Jeannie: 15 Years Later*

MOVIE: *The Garbage Pail Kids*

FAVORITE ACTORS: Humphrey Bogart, Mel Gibson

FAVORITE SPORT: Baseball

FAVORITE COLORS: Blue, gold

FAVORITE MUSIC: Billy Joel, A-ha, Pat Benatar

IDEAL GIRL: "Someone with a nice personality who acts mature."

BIGGEST THRILL: Finding out he got the part on *The Facts of Life*

LITTLE KNOWN FACT: He's ambidextrous, which means he uses both his right *and* left hands.

BEST QUALITY: "I like being able to laugh."

FUTURE GOALS: "My dream is to eventually play a pirate in a movie."

THE THING HE FINDS MOST DIFFICULT: "Keeping up with my schoolwork."

WHERE TO WRITE TO MACKENZIE: Mackenzie Astin
c/o *The Facts of Life*
NBC-TV
3000 West Alameda Avenue
Burbank, CA 91523

SCOTT BAIO

Tall, dark and handsome Scott Baio has been in show business since the age of eleven. Born in Brooklyn, New York, Scott is the youngest of Mario and Rose Baio's three children. He began his career as a model and appeared in numerous television commercials. At the age of fourteen, he was selected from a field of 2,000 actors for the title role in *Bugsy Malone*, and from that film, he went on to star in a string of television shows and movies.

The part which ultimately made brown-eyed Scott a star was Chachi in the TV series *Happy Days*. His popularity soared; he received over five thousand fan letters a week and won the 1981 Youth Achievement Award for his role. After an eight-year run on *Happy Days*, the spin-off *Joanie Loves Chachi* was created for Scott and his co-star Erin Moran.

When that show was canceled, Scott took on several challenging dramatic roles. He played a teenage alcoholic in *The Boy Who Drank Too Much*, and a paraplegic in *Run, Don't Walk*, while his excellent performance in *Stoned* won him a Daytime Emmy nomination.

In addition to acting, multi-talented Scott recorded two albums, *Scott Baio* and *The Boys Are Out Tonight*, and he holds the record for the fastest time on the obstacle course on *Battle of the Network Stars*.

He is happy that his series, *Charles in Charge*, was picked up in syndication because he says, "I always believed in this show." When Scott has some time for fun, he likes playing basketball and baseball.

SCOTT BAIO'S VITAL STATISTICS

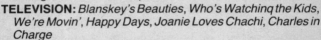

FULL REAL NAME: Scott Baio

BIRTHDATE: September 22, 1961

BIRTHPLACE: Brooklyn, New York

HEIGHT: 5'10"

WEIGHT: 155 lbs.

HAIR: Brown

EYES: Brown

FAMILY: Dad, Mario; mom, Rose; twin siblings, Steven and Stephanie

TELEVISION: *Blanskey's Beauties, Who's Watching the Kids, We're Movin', Happy Days, Joanie Loves Chachi, Charles in Charge*

TV MOVIES: *Stoned, Senior Trip, The Boy Who Drank Too Much, Run, Don't Walk*

FILMS: *Bugsy Malone, Foxes, Skatetown U.S.A., Zapped, I Love New York*

ALBUMS: *Scott Baio, The Boys Are Out Tonight*

FAVORITE FOOD: Italian — especially pizza!

FAVORITE DESSERT: Brownies

FAVORITE SPORTS: Basketball, baseball

FAVORITE CAR: Red Thunderbird

HOBBY: He's collected pigeons since his days in Brooklyn.

BIGGEST THRILL: In 1981, he won the Youth Achievement Award for his role on *Happy Days*

FEELINGS ON FANS: "Being recognized by fans goes with the job and either you love it or you get out. For me, it's definitely a compliment."

FUTURE GOALS: "I don't think about the future. I just think about what's being done now."

WHERE TO WRITE TO SCOTT: Scott Baio
c/o MCA-TV
445 Park Avenue
New York, NY 10022

JASON BATEMAN

At the age of ten, Jason Kent Bateman won the role of James Cooper, Charles Ingalls' adopted son on *Little House on the Prairie*. From his first job, he knew that acting was the life for him. Since that time, he's appeared in numerous TV shows and movies and had the starring part in the feature film *Teen Wolf, Too*, the sequel to Michael J. Fox's movie, *Teen Wolf*.

He says of the film, "It's called Too, as in Also, because it's not exactly a sequel to Michael's movie. I play a cousin of the character Michael played and I'm a teen wolf, too."

Jason was born on January 14, 1969 to Kent and Victoria and grew up in a close-knit family. His older sister, Justine, who plays Mallory on *Family Ties*, has given her brother a lot of guidance. "Justine has really helped me to keep a level head," Jason says. He adds that their father, an actor and director himself, has been their inspiration.

"I really look up to my dad," says the blue-eyed actor. "Besides being my biggest influence, he's also my favorite actor and biggest teacher."

Jason, who appeared on the TV shows *Silver Spoons* and *It's Your Move*, now stars as David Hogan on *Valerie's Family*. Of his character, he says, "David is much more verbal than I am. He can talk his way out of anything."

Jason's future plans are to continue acting. "I love it," he says, smiling.

JASON BATEMAN'S VITAL STATISTICS

FULL REAL NAME: Jason Kent Bateman

NICKNAME: Jake, Mojo

BIRTHDATE: January 14, 1969

BIRTHPLACE: Rye, New York

HEIGHT: 5'11"

WEIGHT: 145 lbs.

HAIR: Brown

EYES: Blue

FAMILY: Producer/director dad, Kent; flight attendant mom, Victoria; actress sister, Justine (*Family Ties*' Mallory)

ACTING DEBUT: He played James Cooper, Charles Ingalls' adopted son in *Little House on the Prairie*

TV SERIES: *Silver Spoons, Little House on the Prairie, It's Your Move, Valerie's Family*

CURRENT RESIDENCE: Woodland Hills, California

FAVORITE CHILDHOOD MEMORY: Living in Utah and skiing every day.

FAVORITE MOVIES: *The Godfather I and II, Midnight Cowboy*

FAVORITE CITY: Manhattan

FAVORITE BANDS: The Police, Van Halen

FAVORITE FOOD: Italian, Japanese

IDEA OF A FUN DATE: "I like going to the movies or maybe just taking a walk and talking so we get to know each other."

BAD HABITS: "Leaving the radio on when I go to bed."

CAR: A black Scirocco Turbo

FAVORITE PASTIMES: Going to the beach, playing football

SELF-DESCRIPTION: Witty, outgoing and intelligent

WHERE TO WRITE TO JASON: Jason Bateman
P.O. Box 333
Woodland Hills, CA 91365

JUSTINE BATEMAN

The first time Justine Bateman stepped in front of the cameras was for a Wheaties commercial. She was sixteen years old and shortly after the commercial aired, she had already landed her role of Mallory Keaton on TV's highly rated show, *Family Ties*.

Justine, born February 19, 1966 in Rye, New York, is the daughter of Kent and Victoria. She is very close to her younger brother, actor Jason Bateman.

When Justine was three, her family moved from Rye to Boston, where they lived for four years. They spent another four years in Salt Lake City before finally settling down in California.

Her early years as an actress combined working with going to school, but ambitious Justine adjusted to the hectic pace easily. She even chose to attend her regular school during hiatus from *Family Ties*, saying, "Otherwise you get swallowed up by the business."

Her role as ditzy Mallory Keaton won Justine two Emmy nominations for supporting actress. In the upcoming movie *Satisfaction* she makes her feature film debut. She says her secret to success stems from what her parents have taught her, which is "to follow through with what you start or don't do it at all."

Justine has many dreams for her future and she is planning on realizing all of them. "Acting is great and I'm good at it," she says. "But if someday people began thinking I wasn't good, then it would be fine. I plan to be a magazine editor or art director, an advertising executive or a movie actress." Talented Justine loves taking chances, and with this kind of determination, she is bound to achieve every goal she sets for herself.

JUSTINE BATEMAN'S VITAL STATISTICS

FULL REAL NAME: Justine Bateman
BIRTHDATE: February 19, 1966
BIRTHPLACE: Rye, New York
HEIGHT: 5'7"
WEIGHT: 115 lbs.
HAIR: Brown
EYES: Blue-gray
CURRENT RESIDENCE: Woodland Hills, California
FAMILY: Producer/director dad, Kent; flight attendant mom, Victoria; actor brother, Jason (David Hogan on *Valerie's Family*)
TELEVISION ROLE: Mallory Keaton on *Family Ties*
MOVIE: *Satisfaction*
CARS: Black BMW, white Alfa Romeo Spider Veloce
FAVORITE SPORTS: Jogging, skiing
FAVORITE FOOD: Chinese
FAVORITE SCHOOL SUBJECTS: French, English
FAVORITE LIPSTICK COLOR: Light shades of red or pink
FAVORITE JEWELRY: Earrings and bangle bracelets
FAVORITE CLOTHES: "I like unique clothes and I do a lot of shopping in thrift stores. I also like to wear my dad's argyle vests from the 50s."
BEST ADVICE SHE EVER RECEIVED: "My parents have taught me and my brother Jason to follow through with what you start or don't do it at all."
FUTURE GOALS: "Nobody realizes that I'm really going to do what I plan," she says with assurance. "That is to be a magazine editor or art director, an advertising executive or a movie actress!"
WHERE TO WRITE TO JUSTINE: Justine Bateman
P.O. Box 333
Woodland Hills, CA 91365

BRIAN BLOOM

At the age of fifteen, crystal-blue-eyed Brian Bloom won a Daytime Emmy Award for Outstanding Young Man for his excellent portrayal of Dusty Donovan on *As The World Turns*. Brian never thought he would win and hadn't even prepared a speech. When his name was announced, he says, "I couldn't believe it!"

Born on June 30, 1970 in Manhasset, New York, Brian took some public speaking courses at the age of eleven, which eventually led to acting classes. Friends of his mother, Linda, told her to get Brian into show business and, accordingly, they met with an agent. Brian had some pictures taken and before the 8 x 10's were even printed, one of his composites was on its way to the casting people of a movie called *Once Upon A Time In America*. The next thing Brian knew, he was auditioning for the role of a street-smart kid and won the part of Young Patsy.

"It was a really great first experience," says Brian. "I went to Italy to shoot it. I worked with the best director, Sergio Leone, and the best actor, Robert DeNiro." Brian appeared in commercials for *Hi-C*, *Jell-O Pudding Pops* and *Quaker Oats* and auditioned for *Search for Tomorrow* and *As The World Turns*. He won parts on both shows, but decided to take the role of Dusty because he felt it was more interesting. Brian recently starred in the NBC-TV movie *Crash Course* with Alyssa Milano and Tina Yothers.

Brian plans on studying architectural engineering in college because, he says, "I want to be an architect. I don't want to get out of acting, though," he adds quickly. "I'd like to do both and I know it can be done."

Brian, who lives in Dix Hills, New York with his family, enjoys spending time with them and his girlfriend Allison Smith on weekends.

BRIAN BLOOM'S VITAL STATISTICS

FULL REAL NAME: Brian Keith Bloom

BIRTHDATE: June 30, 1970

BIRTHPLACE: Manhasset, New York

HEIGHT: 5'11"

WEIGHT: 165 lbs.

HAIR: Dark brown

EYES: Crystal blue

FAMILY: Dad, Richard; mom, Linda; younger brothers, Scott and Mikey

GIRLFRIEND: Allison Smith of *Kate and Allie*

FILMS: *Once Upon A Time In America, Flanagan, The Stuff*

TV MOVIES: *A Different Twist, Crash Course*

TV ROLE: Dusty Donovan on *As The World Turns*

FAVORITE FOOD: Lobster

FAVORITE AUTHOR: Edgar Allen Poe

FAVORITE SPORTS: Basketball, swimming, tennis, skateboarding

FAVORITE COLOR: Blue

FAVORITE SEASON: Fall

FAVORITE SINGERS: Allison Smith, Harry Chapin, Elvis Presley

GREATEST ACHIEVEMENT: At age fifteen, he became the youngest winner of a Daytime Emmy Award for Outstanding Young Man in *As The World Turns*

INSTRUMENT PLAYED: Guitar

BEST QUALITY: "Sincerity and loyalty."

WORST QUALITY: "I use my hands too much when expressing myself."

MOST PRIZED POSSESSIONS: His guitar, customized dirt bike and stereo

WHERE TO WRITE TO BRIAN: Brian Bloom
c/o CBS-TV
51 West 52nd Street
New York, NY 10019

LISA BONET

It is hard for Lisa Bonet to think that people look up to her. "I'm just a regular person," she says. "I haven't done anything *that* big."

In the few years since she entered the entertainment world, Lisa has taken Hollywood by storm. An only child, she was born in San Francisco on November 16, 1967 to a white mother and black father. Her parents divorced when she was just thirteen months old and young Lisa was raised by her Jewish mother, Arlene Boney, in a mostly white community. At school, Lisa remembers she was stuck in the middle. "The black kids called me an Oreo. The white kids didn't talk to me. When I went to temple, I was miserable."

Encouraged by her mother to go into acting, Lisa studied for three years at the Celluloid Actor's Studio in North Hollywood. She won a recurring role on *The Two Of Us* and appeared on *St. Elsewhere*, *Tales from the Dark Side* and *Battle of the Network Stars* before hitting it big on *The Cosby Show*.

At the time she auditioned for the role of Denise Huxtable, her biggest worry was trying to get a date for her high school prom. "I never went," she says. "My problem was solved because I left for New York to begin work on *Cosby*."

For her motion picture debut, Lisa chose to play the steamy role of Epiphany in *Angel Heart*, which originally garnered an X rating. Though many wondered if her love scenes with co-star Mickey Rourke would hurt her wholesome image, Lisa wasn't worried. "I felt obligated to take this part for my career," she says.

Now that Denise Huxtable has gone off to college and Lisa has gotten her own show, *A Different World*, she knows *Angel Heart* hasn't hurt her career at all. Off-screen, Lisa is a very private person who says, "I like being by myself."

LISA BONET'S VITAL STATISTICS

FULL REAL NAME: Lisa Bonet
BIRTHDATE: November 16, 1967
BIRTHPLACE: San Francisco, California
HEIGHT: 5'2"
WEIGHT: 105 lbs.
HAIR: Black
EYES: Dark brown
FAMILY: Lisa's parents were divorced when she was thirteen months old. She is an only child.
FAVORITE ACTOR: Woody Allen
FAVORITE ACTRESSES: Katharine Hepburn, Meryl Streep
FAVORITE SINGER: Prince
FAVORITE FOOD: Vegetarian, pizza with double cheese
FAVORITE DRINK: Perrier
FAVORITE CLOTHES: Oversized sweaters, baggy shorts, hats
FAVORITE LIPSTICK COLOR: All shades of pink
FEELINGS ON HER FANS: "It feels great to get letters. But it really seems crazy that people look up to me."
TELEVISION: *The Cosby Show, A Different World* (spin-off)
MOVIE DEBUT: *Angel Heart*
HOW SHE FEELS ABOUT BEING SUCCESSFUL: "I don't wake up thinking, 'Wow, I'm successful,'" she laughs. "I wake up thinking, 'What am I going to wear today?'"
SELF-DESCRIPTION: "I'm just a regular person. I haven't done anything *that* big!"
WHERE TO WRITE TO LISA: Lisa Bonet
A Different World
c/o NBC-TV
3000 West Alameda Avenue
Burbank, CA 91523

KIRK CAMERON

Kirk Cameron is, without a doubt, the hottest teen star today. As the mischievious Mike Seaver on TV's *Growing Pains*, curly-haired Kirk makes millions of hearts throb every week.

He was born on October 12, 1970 to Robert and Barbara Cameron and began his acting career at age nine. Living in an apartment in the San Fernando Valley, Barbara became good friends with Fran Rich, whose son Adam starred on TV's *Eight is Enough*. She persuaded Barbara to take Kirk and his three younger sisters, Bridgette, Melissa and Candace, to see Adam's agent.

"All four of us were signed up," says Kirk. "And she started sending us on auditions." Kirk's first commercial was for *Super Sugar Crisp* cereal and he worked steadily for the next two years.

At twelve, he began auditioning for roles on TV and appeared in the TV movies *Goliath Awaits*, *Children of the Crossfire* and *Starflight*. He secured parts in Afterschool Specials, the popular shows *Bret Maverick*, *Lou Grant* and *Code Red* and was signed as a regular on the short-lived series *Two Marriages*. Of that show, Kirk says, "It was a fun experience. I'm sorry it didn't last longer."

Before he knew it, *Growing Pains* came his way and he stepped into the role of Mike Seaver with ease. During hiatus from the first season, he made his feature film debut in a small role in *The Best of Times* with Kurt Russell and Robin Williams. He loved working on the movie, and was extremely happy when the lead role in *Like Father, Like Son* was offered to him.

Talented Kirk definitely has a long career ahead of him and he is not worrying about what the future holds. "I don't think about the future. I have so much happening now that I just don't have the time."

KIRK CAMERON'S VITAL STATISTICS

FULL REAL NAME: Kirk Thomas Cameron

BIRTHDATE: October 12, 1970

BIRTHPLACE: Panorama City, California

HEIGHT: 5'9"

WEIGHT: 130 lbs.

HAIR: Light brown

EYES: Hazel

FAMILY: Dad, Robert; mom, Barbara; sisters, Bridgette, Melissa and Candace

PETS: Two snakes and a tarantula

ACTING DEBUT: His first job was in a commercial for *Super Sugar Crisp*

TV SERIES: *Two Marriages, Growing Pains*

FILMS: *The Best of Times, Like Father, Like Son*

MOST PRIZED POSSESSIONS: "My synthesizer and my juke boxes!"

FAVORITE SPORTS: Racquetball, tennis, skiing

FAVORITE MOVIE: *Risky Business*

FAVORITE CLOTHES: Jeans and t-shirts, oversized pants and big shirts

FAVORITE COLOR: Green

FAVORITE CHILDHOOD MEMORY: "When I was 10, my sister fell into a pool and, superman that I was, I jumped in and brought her out."

IDEAL GIRL: "Someone who doesn't wear too much make-up and is down-to-earth."

LITTLE KNOWN FACT: Kirk has never tasted chocolate

WHERE TO MEET KIRK: Santa Monica Beach

WHERE TO WRITE TO KIRK: Kirk Cameron
c/o *Growing Pains*
Warner Bros. Television
4000 Warner Blvd.
Burbank, CA 91522

JOHNNY DEPP

Johnny Depp, the dreamy, brown-eyed star of *21 Jump Street*, stepped into the role of Officer Tommy Hanson with great agility. Fascinated with his character, Johnny says, "I was always getting into mischief as a high-schooler. Now in the show, I'm on the other side of the fence enforcing the law."

Johnny was born on June 9, 1963 in Owensboro, Kentucky. When he was six years old, his family moved to Miramar, Florida where Johnny lived until he left home at age twenty. His parents sold their home in Miramar and now live in Hallendale, Florida where his dad is a Director of Public Works.

Johnny's early childhood was spent learning how to play the guitar. He played in numerous high school bands and after graduation, wanted to try his luck in Hollywood. With his band, The Kids, he headed west. "My friends and I came out here to get a record deal," recalls Johnny. "We'd played some real good shows, but the record companies just weren't signing any new groups. It didn't work out."

Johnny found himself far from home with no money. He got a job selling pens over the telephone and was urged by his friend, actor Nicholas Cage, to try acting.

"I met with an agent who sent me on an audition for the feature film *Nightmare on Elm Street*," explains Johnny. "Two days later, I had the part of Glen and my acting career was launched. Although I enrolled in acting class, I was forced to drop out to accept good roles."

After spots in *Private Resort* and *Platoon*, Johnny auditioned for *21 Jump Street*. "I had the flu that day," he grins. "But it helped my concentration. I got the part." Although Johnny wants to continue acting, he'd also like to go back to his first love, music, someday.

JOHNNY DEPP'S VITAL STATISTICS

FULL REAL NAME: John Christopher Depp

BIRTHDATE: June 9, 1963

BIRTHPLACE: Owensboro, Kentucky

HEIGHT: 5'9"

WEIGHT: 147 lbs.

HAIR: Dark brown

EYES: Brown

HOMETOWN: Miramar, Florida

CURRENT RESIDENCE: Los Angeles, California

FIRST AMBITION: To become a singer

FIRST BAND: The Kids

FAVORITE CHILDHOOD MEMORY: "Living in Miramar, Florida was great and forming my own band called The Kids."

MOVIES: *Nightmare On Elm Street*, *Private Resort*, *Platoon*

TV MOVIE: *Slow Burn* (Cable movie)

TELEVISION ROLE: Officer Tommy Hanson on *21 Jump Street*

INSTRUMENT PLAYED: Guitar

EARLY JOB: Selling pens over the telephone

BEST FRIEND: Actor Nicholas Cage

BEST EXPERIENCE AS AN ACTOR: "Getting the part of Glen in *Nightmare On Elm Street*. That launched my acting career."

WORST EXPERIENCE AS AN ACTOR: "*Private Resort* was one of the worst movies ever made," he says.

HIS FEELINGS ON HIS CHARACTER, TOMMY HANSON: "I know where the show is coming from," says Johnny. "I reveal how scared, vulnerable and prone to making mistakes my character is as a police officer."

FUTURE GOALS: "I definitely want to get back into music."

WHERE TO WRITE TO JOHNNY: Johnny Depp
c/o Fox Broadcasting Co.
10201 West Pico Blvd.
Los Angeles,
California 90035

ANDREA ELSON

Andrea Elson first realized her love for acting at age eleven when she played the lead in a sixth grade production of *Alice in Wonderland*. "The first time I was ever on stage it felt so natural and right, I knew I had to be an actress," says green-eyed Andrea.

Born on March 6, 1969 in New York City, she grew up traveling because of her father's job in advertising. Before she was ten years old, she had lived in New York, Chicago, San Diego and Los Angeles. While in San Diego, Andrea got an agent and won the first part she auditioned for. It was for a commercial, and from then on, one acting job followed another.

"I thought it was so easy because every audition I went on, I got the job," she says. "But when things began to slow down, I realized that I wasn't going to keep going at that pace." She landed guest-starring parts on *Simon and Simon* and *Silver Spoons* and a co-starring role in the series *Whiz Kids*.

When that ended, she found herself auditioning again. At the audition for *Alf*, it was her braces that helped her get the role. "During my first audition, someone asked if my braces could come off," Andrea recalls. "I said if it meant that I'd get the part, then they could definitely come off. Then someone else said, 'Hey, the kid has braces. I love it!' "

Andrea, whose braces have since come off, is grateful for the opportunity to play such a terrific role on one of the biggest hit shows on television. When she is asked if she'd like to change anything in her life, she says with confidence, "No, I wouldn't want to mess with the past at all because things might not have worked out as great as they have!"

ANDREA ELSON'S VITAL STATISTICS

FULL REAL NAME: Andrea Elson
BIRTHDATE: March 6, 1969
BIRTHPLACE: New York, NY
HEIGHT: 5'6"
WEIGHT: 105 lbs.
HAIR: Dark blonde
EYES: Green
CURRENT RESIDENCE: Los Angeles, California

FAMILY: Dad, Stephen; mom, Elinor; older sister, Samantha
PET: Dog, Weimaraner named Gunnar
TV ROLE: Lynn Tanner on *Alf*
TELEVISION: *Whiz Kids*. Guest appearances on *Simon and Simon, Silver Spoons*
FIRST ACTING BREAK: She played Alice in a sixth grade production of *Alice in Wonderland*
FIRST LOVE: Acting
SECOND LOVE: Traveling
BIGGEST INFLUENCE ON HER LIFE: Her parents
SELF-DESCRIPTION: "I can be serious but I love to have fun!"
FEELINGS ON ACTING: "The first time I was ever on stage it felt so natural and right, I knew I had to be an actress."
BIGGEST THRILL: "Two years ago, I spent a month in Europe traveling through eight countries. It was a wonderful experience."
FUTURE GOALS: To continue acting
WHERE TO WRITE TO ANDREA: Andrea Elson
c/o *Alf*
NBC-TV
3000 West Alameda Ave.
Burbank, CA 91523

MICHAEL J. FOX

Talented Michael J. Fox has reached superstardom in both television and motion pictures. Not only does he star on TV's *Family Ties* each week, but he is also one of the hottest movie stars on the silver screen.

He was born Michael Andrew Fox in Edmonton, Canada on June 9, 1961. His parents, Bill and Phyllis, moved their ten-year-old son, his three sisters and brother to Vancouver, British Columbia after his dad, a sergeant in the Canadian Army Signal Corps, retired. It was during these years that Michael developed his desire to act. At fifteen, he successfully auditioned for the role of a ten-year-old in a series called *Leo and Me*. Gaining attention as a bright new star in Canadian television and movies, Michael realized his love for acting when he appeared on stage in *The Shadow Box*.

At eighteen, he moved to Los Angeles and was offered a few roles in television shows. But early acting success ended fast when the roles stopped coming. For a while he survived on boxes of macaroni and cheese. Then his agent called to tell him that he got the part of Alex Keaton on the TV series *Family Ties*, and Michael's luck changed. After starring in the feature film *Teen Wolf*, and TV movies *High School U.S.A.* and *Poison Ivy*, he was offered the role of Marty McFly in the sleeper hit of 1985, *Back to the Future*. Regarding the period when he filmed the movie and *Family Ties* at the same time, Michael says, "I look back at it now as a lot of fun and even though it was exhausting, it was sure worth it."

Michael repeated his back-to-back filming schedule for his latest movies, *Light of Day*, *The Secret of My Success* and *Bright Lights, Big City* and he says he enjoys being "in a position now where they're coming to me." He won an Emmy Award two years in a row for his portrayal of Alex Keaton. "What's ahead can only get better," says Michael. "I have everything I want right now."

MICHAEL J. FOX'S VITAL STATISTICS

FULL REAL NAME: Michael Andrew Fox (the "J" was added later)

BIRTHDATE: June 9, 1961

BIRTHPLACE: Edmonton, Alberta, Canada

HEIGHT: 5'4½"

WEIGHT: 120 lbs.

HAIR: Brown

EYES: Blue

FAMILY: Dad, Bill; mom, Phyllis; sisters, Kelli, Karen, Jacki; brother, Steven

ACTING DEBUT: His first job when he was fifteen years old was playing a ten-year-old in the Canadian TV series *Leo And Me*.

TV SHOWS: *Leo And Me*, *Palmerstown, U.S.A.*, *Family Ties*, Guest appearances on *Lou Grant*, *Family*, *Trapper John MD*

TV MOVIES: *Letters From Frank*, *High School U.S.A.*, *Poison Ivy*

FILMS: *Midnight Madness*, *Class of 1984*, *Teen Wolf*, *Back to the Future*, *Light of Day*, *Secret of My Success*, *Bright Lights, Big City*

FAVORITE FOOD: Linguini with clam sauce, fresh fruit

FAVORITE COLOR: Khaki

FAVORITE COLOGNE: Polo by Ralph Lauren

FAVORITE TIME OF DAY: Midnight

FAVORITE SPORT: Ice hockey

IDEAL GIRL: "A sense of humor is very important to me," he says. "I could definitely fall in love with a girl who could make me laugh."

BIGGEST THRILL: Winning two Emmy Awards for his role on *Family Ties*

PET PEEVE: People who are rude to each other

WHERE TO WRITE TO MICHAEL: Michael J. Fox
c/o *Family Ties*
NBC-TV
3000 West Alameda Ave.
Burbank, CA 91523

TRACEY GOLD

Tracey Gold says that of all the roles she's played, Carol Seaver on *Growing Pains* is her favorite. "I love playing Carol because I'm really different from her even though I put a lot of myself into the character," explains Tracey, who was born into a family of over-achievers.

She is very close to her parents, Bonnie and Harry (who is her manager), and younger sisters, Brandy, Jessie and Missy (who played Katie on the TV series *Benson*). Tracey's career began at age four when her dad went on a soft drink commercial audition and she tagged along. "The man in charge of casting the commercial must have thought I was one of the kids trying out because he said, 'Finally, they sent me the right kid!'" remembers Tracey, laughing.

Since her first job, she has appeared in fifteen TV movies, two feature films, *The Best of Times* and *Shoot the Moon*, and two television series. For her performances in *Goodnight Beantown* and *Growing Pains*, she was awarded the Youth-in-Film Award for Best Actress.

Tracey, who enjoys meeting fans and signing autographs, says, "I've never looked at myself or what I do as being better than anyone else. My parents just taught us to be normal kids. At home, my sisters and I forget about show business. That's just how we were raised."

Tracey graduated from high school in June, 1987 and doesn't plan on going to college. Instead, she wants to concentrate on her career as an actress. "I'd like to be involved with feature films," she reflects. "I want to become the best actress I can!"

TRACEY GOLD'S VITAL STATISTICS

FULL REAL NAME: Tracey Goldstein
BIRTHDATE: May 16, 1969
BIRTHPLACE: New York City
HEIGHT: 5'2"
WEIGHT: 108 lbs.
HAIR: Light brown
EYES: Brown
FAMILY: Dad, Harry; mom, Bonnie; three sisters, Missy, Brandy and Jessie
FAVORITE SINGER: Bruce Springsteen
FAVORITE DRINK: Tab
FAVORITE FOOD: Pizza
FAVORITE COLOR: Pink
FAVORITE TV SHOWS: *The Cosby Show, Family Ties*
FAVORITE SPORTS: Ice skating, swimming, gymnastics
PETS: Two cats, E.T. and Sam, one dog, Rachel
TV SERIES: *Shirley, Goodnight Beantown, Growing Pains*
TV MOVIES: *Another Woman's Child, Who Will Love My Children?*
FILMS: *Shoot the Moon, The Best of Times* (with Kirk Cameron)
MOST THRILLING EXPERIENCE: "The day my sister Jessie was born, I was in the delivery room," she says. "That was a really incredible experience for me."
HOW SHE FEELS ABOUT FANS: "I like being recognized. I think it's great when people come up to me. That's basically why I'm an actress."
FUTURE GOALS: "I'd like to be involved with feature films. I want to become the best actress I can!"
WHERE TO WRITE TO TRACEY: Tracey Gold
c/o *Growing Pains*
Warner Bros. Television
4000 Warner Blvd.
Burbank, CA 91522

BENJI GREGORY

Getting involved with acting was natural for adorable Benji Gregory, who plays Brian Tanner on TV's smash hit *Alf*. His father, uncle and sister were all actors and his grandmother is his agent.

Blue-eyed Benji was born in Encino, California to Manny and Patti Gregory and he has one older sister and one younger brother. As a veteran of dozens of commercials, Benji literally grew up before the camera. At the age of five, he began auditioning for television and won numerous parts. His first acting job was in an episode of *Fantasy Island* and he followed that with guest-starring parts on *The A-Team*, *T. J. Hooker*, *Amazing Stories* and *The Twilight Zone*. He also appeared in a TV pilot, *Fenster Hall*, a Disney movie, *Mr. Boogidy*, a TV movie, *The Last Run*, and the feature film *Jumping Jack Flash*.

Benji, who says working on *Alf* is fun, loves hanging out in the clubhouse he and his dad built in their back yard in Thousand Oaks, California. He also enjoys playing with his pets, three dogs, two birds and seven cats.

When Benji isn't on the set or doing his schoolwork, he likes adding to his three favorite collections of rocks, shells and Garbage Pail Kids cards.

Looking to his future, this bright nine-year-old has things right on track. "Sure I want to be an actor," he says, then adds with a grin, "otherwise I have to get a job!"

BENJI GREGORY'S VITAL STATISTICS

FULL REAL NAME: Benjamin Gregory

BIRTHDATE: May 26, 1978

BIRTHPLACE: Encino, California

HEIGHT: 4'8"

WEIGHT: 85 lbs.

HAIR: Sandy blond

EYES: Blue

FAMILY: Dad, Manny; mom, Patti; sister, Becky; brother, Matthew

PETS: Three dogs, two birds and seven cats

TV ROLE: Brian Tanner on *Alf*

CURRENT RESIDENCE: Thousand Oaks, California

FAVORITE FOOD: McDonald's Chicken McNuggets

FAVORITE WAY TO SPEND FREE TIME: Hanging out in the clubhouse he and his dad built in their back yard

HE LIKES TO COLLECT: Rocks, shells and Garbage Pail Kids cards

HOW HE FEELS ABOUT WORKING ON *ALF*: "It's fun. Alf teases me a lot and he talks too much," says Benji, laughing.

TELEVISION: *Fantasy Island, The A-Team, T.J. Hooker, Amazing Stories, The Twilight Zone, Fenster Hall*

TELEVISION MOVIES: *Disney movie: Mr. Boogidy, The Last Run*

MOVIE: *Jumping Jack Flash*

SELF-DESCRIPTION: "I'm real shy!"

WHERE TO WRITE TO BENJI: Benji Gregory
c/o *Alf*
NBC-TV
3000 West Alameda Avenue
Burbank, CA 91523

SCOTT GRIMES

Scott Grimes never planned on an acting career, yet in only a few short years he's appeared on Broadway, in movies and on television. He was born on July 9, 1971 in Lowell, Massachusetts and his first acting role was in a local production of *Oliver* at age nine. He was such a natural that his director strongly encouraged young Scott to try out on Broadway. With that advice in mind, the Grimes family went to New York. Only two days after their arrival, Scott auditioned for the role of Pepe in *Nine* and won it. He played the part for ten months and was next offered a role opposite Anthony Newley in the musical *Chaplin*.

His introduction to television soon followed. First he played Art Carney's grandson in the TV movie *Doctors Story* and then opposite Mickey Rooney in *It Came Upon A Midnight Clear*. He guest-starred on *Hotel, Twilight Zone* and *Who's The Boss?* and starred on the weekly TV series *Nothing is Easy*.

Even though Scott maintains a very busy schedule, he still manages to donate time to charities, helping to raise money for the American Cancer Society and the AIDS Research Foundation. Recently, he signed a five-year contract with A & M Records. "I do all kinds of songs. Ballads and old songs and I'm just getting into new songs," says Scott, whose first album was produced by Richard Carpenter.

For fun, this health-conscious young man enjoys tennis and bowling. He is best friends with fellow actors Sean and Mackenzie Astin and just started to experiment with making his own short films. Of his future, brown-eyed Scott says, "I'd like to do another TV series, but I really want to get into films and continue singing. Maybe I'll even go back to Broadway!"

SCOTT GRIMES' VITAL STATISTICS

FULL REAL NAME: Scott Grimes

BIRTHDATE: July 9, 1971

BIRTHPLACE: Lowell, Massachusetts

HEIGHT: 5'5"

WEIGHT: 125 lbs.

HAIR: Red

EYES: Brown

FAMILY: Dad, Richard; mom, Pamela; older sister, Heather

PETS: Two dogs and two cats

BEST FRIENDS: Sean and Mackenzie Astin

THEATRE CREDITS: Scott appeared on Broadway in *Nine* and played opposite Anthony Newley in the musical *Chaplin*

MOVIE: *Critters*

TV MOVIES: *Doctors Story*, *It Came Upon A Midnight Clear*, *The Night They Saved Christmas*

TELEVISION: *Nothing is Easy*, Guest appearances on *Hotel*, *Twilight Zone* and *Who's The Boss?*

RECORDING DEBUT: Scott signed a five-year recording contract with A & M Records. His debut album will be released soon.

FAVORITE SINGER: Bruce Springsteen

FAVORITE SCHOOL SUBJECT: Science

FAVORITE SPORTS: Bowling, tennis

FAVORITE FOOD: Hamburgers and fries

IDEAL GIRL: "I like a girl with a good sense of humor as well as a good personality."

FUTURE GOALS: "Just to keep working on new projects. I love to work."

WHERE TO WRITE TO SCOTT: Scott Grimes
c/o CBS-TV
7800 Beverly Blvd.
Hollywood, CA 90036

NANCY McKEON

Nancy McKeon started her career by tagging along with her mom and big brother, Philip, to open calls for child models. Nancy, who was born in Westbury, New York to Don and Barbara McKeon, began modeling baby clothes for the Sears catalogue at the age of two and she and her brother did over sixty-five commercials in seven years.

She appeared briefly on the soap operas *The Secret Storm* and *Another World* and says those early days of her career "were a blast!" All that suddenly changed when Philip won his role on the TV series *Alice* and the McKeons moved to Los Angeles. Once settled in California, Nancy began going on auditions, but didn't get anything right away. "It was very discouraging," she says. "It was like I had to start all over again."

Her first real acting break came when she did the short-lived TV series *Stone* and guested on *Starsky and Hutch*. When the producers of *Facts of Life* spotted Nancy's performance as the street-wise girl in a pilot called *Dusty*, they knew they had the actress they were looking for to play Jo. Says Nancy, "I'm the total opposite of Jo. She tells you what's on her mind and I keep a lot of stuff inside. I'm basically very shy."

Nancy has starred in the television movies *High School U.S.A.*, *Poison Ivy*, *This Child Is Mine* and *The Greater Alarm* and has provided the voices for animated shows like *Puppy's Great Adventure*. When she has some free time, she loves to shop, play racquetball and cook. She also likes spending time with her brother and says, "My dream is to do a movie with Philip one day."

For this talented young actress, who is affectionately nicknamed Faucet Face because she cries easily, acting is very important. And she plans to stick with it for a long time to come.

NANCY MCKEON'S VITAL STATISTICS

FULL REAL NAME: Nancy McKeon

BIRTHDATE: April 4, 1966

BIRTHPLACE: Westbury, New York

NICKNAME: Faucet Face because she cries easily

HEIGHT: 5'5"

WEIGHT: 125 lbs.

HAIR: Brown

EYES: Hazel

FAMILY: Dad, Don; mom, Barbara; brother, Philip

FIRST ACTING BREAK: *Stone*, a police drama

TELEVISION: *The Secret Storm, Another World, Facts of Life*

TV MOVIES: *High School, U.S.A., Poison Ivy, A Question of Love, This Child is Mine, The Greater Alarm*

FAVORITE FOOD: Anything Italian, especially veal cutlet parmigiana

FAVORITE CITY: New York

FAVORITE SINGER: Lionel Richie

FAVORITE PASTIMES: Aerobic and jazz dance, cooking, running, window-shopping

FAVORITE ACTORS: Richard Gere, Al Pacino, Dustin Hoffman, Tom Selleck

PET PEEVE: Wild parties

WHAT SHE LIKES ABOUT HERSELF: "My best feature is my legs."

BEST FRIENDS: *Facts of Life* co-star Lisa Whelchel, her brother Philip

CURRENT RESIDENCE: Hollywood Hills, CA

LITTLE KNOWN FACT: She attends Mass every Sunday

WHERE TO WRITE TO NANCY: Nancy McKeon
c/o NBC-TV
3000 West Alameda Ave.
Burbank, CA 91505

ALYSSA MILANO

When Alyssa Milano went to see *Annie* on Broadway at age eight, she decided that it was something she had to be part of. Brown-eyed Alyssa, who turned fifteen on December 19, went to an open call of the hit Broadway play and was one of four to be offered a role. Her professional career began with a bang as this bright star won almost every role she auditioned for including stage plays *Jane Eyre*, *Tender Offer* and *All Night Long* and movies *Old Enough* and *Commando* with Arnold Schwarzenegger.

Then *Who's The Boss?* came along and this talented young lady knocked down competition from every juvenile actress in Hollywood and won the role of Tony Danza's daughter, Samantha Micelli, hands down. "I'm so lucky to be on the show because the entire cast has so much love for each other," Alyssa smiles. "Tony (Danza) is great. He's always making me laugh!" Recently, Alyssa starred in the TV movie *Crash Course*.

To get away from show business, Alyssa enjoys spending time with her family and friends like fellow actor Scott Grimes. She plays the flute and piano to relax and loves to sing, dance and write poetry.

Her parents, she feels, have helped her handle everything with ease. "My parents are really cool," she says with a smile. "Whenever I need advice I ask them, even when it comes to boys!"

Her style, she admits, is to "take it all day to day. I want to go to college, but I also hope to continue acting. I just can't imagine doing anything else!"

ALYSSA MILANO'S VITAL STATISTICS

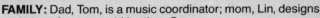

FULL REAL NAME: Alyssa Jayne Milano

NICKNAME: Lyssa

BIRTHDATE: December 19, 1972

BIRTHPLACE: Brooklyn, New York

HEIGHT: 5'1"

WEIGHT: 85 lbs.

HAIR: Brown

EYES: Brown

FAMILY: Dad, Tom, is a music coordinator; mom, Lin, designs clothes; four-year-old brother, Cory

FIRST AMBITION: To be a hairstylist

TV ROLE: Samantha Micelli on *Who's The Boss?*

FAVORITE COLOR: Blue

FAVORITE BAND: The Beastie Boys

FAVORITE CITIES: New York and Los Angeles

FAVORITE FOOD: Fritos, french fries without ketchup, Pepperidge Farm cookies and "my mom's Italian cooking!"

WHAT SHE LIKES BEST ABOUT HERSELF: "I don't give up!"

WHAT SHE LIKES LEAST ABOUT HERSELF: "I hate losing."

PET: Dog named Pucci

THE BIGGEST INFLUENCE ON HER LIFE: "My parents. They encourage me."

SELF-DESCRIPTION: Determined

FAVORITE QUOTE: Before Alyssa moved with her family from New York to California, her Aunt Sissy told her, "It's nice to be important, but it's important to always be nice."

WHERE TO WRITE TO ALYSSA: Alyssa Milano
c/o *Who's The Boss?*
Embassy Television
Sunset-Gower Studios
1438 N. Gower Street
Hollywood, CA 90028

JEREMY MILLER

At the age of six, Jeremy Miller began taking singing and acting lessons. The enthusiastic youngster was a natural and his acting teacher decided to send his snapshots around to a list of agents. "I went on six interviews and got a McDonald's commercial," says Jeremy. "But then I went on another 350 auditions and didn't work for a year and a half."

What helped Jeremy's career was that his agent stopped sending him on commercial auditions. "I was in my agent's office and I read a scene from a Steven Spielberg script," remembers Jeremy. "The agency was so impressed with my delivery that they started sending me on theatrical interviews."

Almost immediately, Jeremy was cast in TV shows, *Charles in Charge*, *Punky Brewster*, *Pryor's Place* and *Diff'rent Strokes*. He had a small part in the TV movie *Deceptions* and is also the voice of Linus in the Peanuts specials. But his big break came when he won the role of Ben Seaver on *Growing Pains*. He finds playing the younger brother of Kirk Cameron and Tracey Gold a lot of fun. "I love being part of *Growing Pains*," he says. "It's nice that Tracey is like a big sister because I never had a sister that looked out for me."

When he isn't working on the show or going to school, Jeremy likes playing video games and watching TV. He is very close to his younger brother, Joshua, and encouraged Joshua to try acting. Jeremy's little brother took his advice and made his own television debut last season in a small part on *Growing Pains*. As for Jeremy, he recently made his movie debut in *Emanon* and looks forward to a long career in acting.

JEREMY MILLER'S VITAL STATISTICS

FULL REAL NAME: Jeremy Miller

BIRTHDATE: October 21, 1976

BIRTHPLACE: Alhambra, California

HEIGHT: 5′2″

WEIGHT: 100 lbs.

HAIR: It's blond, but is dyed brown for the show

EYES: Light brown

FAMILY: Mom, Sonja; two brothers (younger brother, Joshua, also acts)

CURRENT RESIDENCE: Alhambra, California

TV ROLE: Ben Seaver on *Growing Pains*

EARLIEST INTEREST IN ACTING: "I guess I was about three. I was watching *The Brady Bunch* on TV and copied what Bobby, the youngest brother, did. My mom saw me and asked me if I wanted to be an actor and I said that I did."

TELEVISION: *Charles in Charge, Punky Brewster, Pryor's Place, Diff'rent Strokes, Growing Pains*

TV MOVIE: *Deceptions*

MOVIE: *Emanon*

FAVORITE SPORT: Swimming

FAVORITE WAY TO SPEND FREE TIME: Watching TV and playing video games

FAVORITE SCHOOL SUBJECT: Reading

BIGGEST THRILL: He sang *Twist and Shout* in a show at Knotts Berry Farm called *Never Too Young To Rock*

BIGGEST INFLUENCE ON HIS LIFE: "My mom!"

FUTURE GOALS: "I want to continue acting!"

WHERE TO WRITE TO JEREMY: Jeremy Miller
c/o *Growing Pains*
Warner Bros. Television
4000 Warner Blvd.
Burbank, CA 91522

MICHAEL PARE

The sizzling star of *Houston Knights* is devastatingly handsome Michael Pare. Born on October 9, 1958 in Brooklyn, New York, Michael was raised in Tarrytown and went to high school in Michigan. He didn't decide to become an actor until he was twenty-two.

Michael graduated from the Culinary Institute of America and his first ambition was to become a chef. He even worked for a while as a chef at the Tavern on the Green restaurant in New York City. It was there that an agent "discovered" him and encouraged the 6'2" tall, hazel-eyed young man to pursue a career in acting. After he did a little modeling, Michael got his big TV break on *The Greatest American Hero*. Quickly catching on, he went on to star in the films *Eddie and the Cruisers*, *Streets of Fire*, *The Philadelphia Experiment* and *The Women's Club*.

As Joey La Fiamma on *Houston Knights*, Michael plays a slick Chicago cop out of place in Houston, Texas. "The show is basically the story of two cops," he says. "It focuses on Michael Beck and me and follows our characters through their conflicts."

In his spare time, Michael likes to go fishing, work out and box. "Boxing teaches me movement," he notes. "I take boxing lessons and like to do stunts. As a matter of fact, I do my own stunts on the show."

Married to former model Marissa Roebuck, Michael enjoys cooking, astronomy and whittling. Besides his weekly TV show, gorgeous Michael can also be seen on the big screen in *World Gone Mad* and *Stoner*, which is directed by Sylvester Stallone. Of this film, Michael says, "It's a cross between *Cobra* and *Streets of Fire*."

MICHAEL PARE'S VITAL STATISTICS

FULL REAL NAME: Michael Pare

BIRTHDATE: October 9, 1958

BIRTHPLACE: Brooklyn, New York

HEIGHT: 6'2"

WEIGHT: 175 lbs.

HAIR: Brown

EYES: Blue/green

BACKGROUND: Irish-American

FAMILY: Michael comes from a large family. He has three brothers and six sisters.

MARITAL STATUS: Married to former model/interior designer Marissa Roebuck

FIRST ACTING BREAK: He was a series regular on *The Greatest American Hero*

FILMS: *Eddie and the Cruisers, Streets of Fire, The Philadelphia Experiment, The Women's Club*

LATEST FILM: *World Gone Wild*

TV SERIES: *The Greatest American Hero, Houston Knights*

FIRST AMBITION: To be a chef

FAVORITE HOBBIES: Cooking, astronomy, whittling

FAVORITE SPORTS: Boxing, fishing

HOW HE STAYS IN SHAPE: Exercising every day and lifting weights

LITTLE KNOWN FACT: He does his own stunts on *Houston Knights.*

FUTURE GOALS: He likes being back on television, but wants to make more movies, too.

FEELINGS ON *HOUSTON KNIGHTS*: "I started out as a Chicago cop who was transferred to Houston, Texas. My partner is an ex-football player/cowboy played by Michael Beck. We complain a lot, moan a lot. But you might find more humor in the show this year."

WHERE TO WRITE TO MICHAEL: Michael Pare
c/o CBS-TV
7800 Beverly Blvd.
Hollywood, CA 90036

PAT PETERSEN

At the ripe age of twelve, Pat Petersen won his role of Michael Fairgate on *Knots Landing* and has literally grown up on television. Born in Los Angeles, Pat always dreamed of going into show business. He began acting when he was eight. "My two older brothers were on a football team and they did a commercial," says Pat. By accompanying them on auditions, he also began appearing in commercials and a variety of Afterschool Specials followed. He landed plum roles in three movies, *Cold River*, *Little Dragons* and *Alligators*, before going on an interview for a new show called *Knots Landing*.

"It was just a basic interview for a pilot," he says. "I don't think anyone expected it to be the hit it has become." After nine years on the show, Pat says he feels "fortunate to work with the most talented and professional group of actors on prime-time television."

In his spare time, blond-haired Pat enjoys tennis, golf, surfing and skiing. He loves reading his fan mail and always finds the time to answer it. "I feel like everyone who writes to me is really just like me," he notes. "When I was growing up, I would've liked the person I was writing to to answer me personally. And that's just what I try to do. It might take some time, but I get around to mostly all the letters."

Though Pat wants to stay on *Knots Landing*, he is looking forward to a career in movies. "I'd love to go into all aspects of the entertainment business, particularly directing and writing," he says. Of his acting, he confides, "I don't know my limits yet as an actor, but I'm always learning and growing."

PAT PETERSEN'S VITAL STATISTICS

FULL REAL NAME: Patrick John Petersen

BIRTHDATE: August 9, 1966

BIRTHPLACE: Los Angeles, California

HEIGHT: 5'9"

WEIGHT: 140 lbs.

HAIR: Blond

EYES: Blue

FAMILY: Dad, John; mom, Carol; brothers, Chris, Mike and Tommy

CURRENT RESIDENCE: Westwood, California

TV SERIES: *Knots Landing*

FILMS: *Cold River*, *Little Dragons*, *Alligators*

INSTRUMENTS PLAYED: Piano, guitar

FAVORITE SPORTS: Golf, tennis, surfing, skiing

FAVORITE SINGERS: Phil Collins, The Rolling Stones

FAVORITE ACTORS: Henry Fonda, Spencer Tracy, James Stewart

FAVORITE COLOR: Light blue

FAVORITE VACATION SPOT: Hawaii

FAVORITE FOOD: Chinese

IDEAL GIRL: "Just friendly and fun to be around, not too terribly shy, but not too outgoing either. I guess just someone I could have fun with."

IDEA OF A FUN DATE: "I like to stay home and watch movies. Maybe have a pizza once in a while. When I go out, I like doing stupid things like going bowling or playing miniature golf."

WHAT HE LIKES BEST ABOUT HIMSELF: "I care for others and like sharing my good luck with others."

WHAT HE LIKES LEAST ABOUT HIMSELF: "I don't push myself to do the things I don't want to do."

WHERE TO WRITE TO PAT: Pat Petersen
c/o *Knots Landing*
CBS-TV
7800 Beverly Blvd.
Los Angeles, CA 90036

BRIAN ROBBINS

Brian Robbins plays Eric Mardian, the sarcastic, leather-jacketed rebel on the hit TV series *Head of the Class*. Brian, who was born in Brooklyn, New York to a theatrical agent mom and a character actor dad, always had show business in his blood.

He studied acting in New York with a class of students between the ages of sixteen and twenty. "I met my good friend Ralph Macchio in that class," says Brian. "And we did a lot of work together. Ralph was like my adopted brother."

Upon moving to California, Brian was very excited to learn he'd won the role of Eric on *Head of the Class*. "Eric is a very interesting character," notes handsome Brian. "Even though we don't have that much in common, I can relate to him. In high school, I was a little sarcastic, but Eric is more of a rebel than I ever was."

Brian is a very easy-going guy who likes to have fun when he has time off. He gets along very well with everyone on the set of the show and likes to shoot a few baskets to keep in shape. "I also like to work out," he offers. "But I could play basketball for hours."

This lover of Bruce Springsteen music doesn't have a steady girlfriend right now, but is looking for love. His favorite kind of girl is "someone who has a lot of happening in her own life — so much that she has to find time for me."

Talented Brian's future looks very bright. He plans on acting for a long time and says with a smile, "I'm looking forward to getting into the movies!"

BRIAN ROBBINS' VITAL STATISTICS

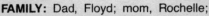

FULL REAL NAME: Brian Robbins

BIRTHDATE: November 22, 1964

BIRTHPLACE: Brooklyn, New York

HEIGHT: 5'10"

WEIGHT: 150 lbs.

HAIR: Brown

EYES: Brown

FAMILY: Dad, Floyd; mom, Rochelle; brother, Marc; sister, Sheryl

TV ROLE: Eric Mardian on *Head of the Class*

BEST FRIENDS: Sam Jones, Tom Wopat, Ralph Macchio

FAVORITE SHOWS: *Moonlighting, Cheers*

FAVORITE FOOD: Italian

FAVORITE SPORTS: Basketball, baseball

FAVORITE ACTRESSES: Jessica Lange, Debra Winger

FAVORITE BAND: U2

FAVORITE COLORS: Red, white, black

FAVORITE SINGERS: Bruce Springsteen, Frank Sinatra

IDEAL GIRL: "Someone fun with an outgoing personality."

IDEA OF A GREAT DATE: "Something romantic like taking a drive to the beach, just the two of us."

FIRST AMBITION: To play professional baseball

FAVORITE CHILDHOOD MEMORY: "When the Mets won the World Series in 1969."

FUTURE GOALS: "I hope one day to play a cop like Serpico because I'd love to get into the movies."

HOW HE FEELS ABOUT SUCCESS: "It's weird to go into a grocery store and pick up a magazine and whoa, you're in it."

WHERE TO WRITE TO BRIAN: Brian Robbins
c/o *Head of the Class*
ABC-TV
2040 Avenue of the Stars
Los Angeles, CA 90067

RICKY SCHRODER

Ricky Schroder began acting at the tender age of eight in the tearjerker *The Champ* and has been in the public eye most of his life. The role won him the Golden Globe Award for Best New Male Star of 1979 and secured him a name in Hollywood.

He was born Richard Bartlett Schroder, Jr. on April 13, 1970 in Staten Island, New York. His parents, Richard, Sr. and Diane, and older sister, Dawn, have always been very supportive of Ricky's career. In fact, he credits his mother with getting the ball rolling for him in show business. At three months of age, he began appearing in TV commercials and magazine ads and by the time he was eight, he had done more than fifty advertisements.

It was after he appeared in *The Champ* that roles started pouring in, and from 1979 to 1983, Ricky starred in a string of movies including *Two Kinds of Love*, *The Earthling* and *The Last Flight of Noah's Ark*. In 1983, he auditioned for the TV series *Silver Spoons*, and won the lead part of Rick Stratton.

For two years, Ricky found himself living in Connecticut, where his family had moved from Staten Island, and working in California on the series. In 1985, the Schroder family decided it was time to move to California and they settled in a beautiful home in Calabasas. "I really like the weather out here, but I will always love the rustic scenery in Connecticut," says Ricky, who likes visiting his favorite state as often as he can.

In 1986, Ricky celebrated his 16th birthday by treating himself to a white Porsche 944 sports car. Later in the year, he sadly learned *Silver Spoons* was canceled. He spent the summer of 1987 filming a new TV movie titled *Too Young The Hero* and discovered he definitely wants to continue acting in the future. "I love to work," he smiles.

RICKY SCHRODER'S VITAL STATISTICS

FULL REAL NAME: Richard Bartlett Schroder, Jr.

BIRTHDATE: April 13, 1970

BIRTHPLACE: Staten Island, New York

HEIGHT: 5′9″

WEIGHT: 135 lbs.

HAIR: Blond

EYES: Blue

FAMILY: Dad, Richard; mom, Diane; older sister, Dawn

FIRST ACTING BREAK: Ricky made his show business debut at the age of three months doing TV commercials

FILMS: *The Champ, The Earthling, The Last Flight of Noah's Ark*

TV MOVIES: *Two Kinds of Love, A Reason to Live, Too Young The Hero*

TELEVISION SERIES: *Silver Spoons*

BIGGEST THRILL: Winning a Golden Globe Award for Best New Male Star of 1979 for his role in *The Champ*

FAVORITE FOOD: Italian

FAVORITE SINGERS: Michael Jackson, Pet Shop Boys, Mr. Mister

FAVORITE SNACKS: Ice cream, popcorn

FAVORITE ACTOR: Eddie Murphy

FAVORITE ACTRESS: Jessica Lange

FAVORITE COLORS: Blue, green and yellow

FAVORITE CHILDHOOD MEMORY: Swimming in the ocean with his dad

FAVORITE HOBBIES: Collecting coins and toy trains

CAR: White Porsche 944

IDEAL GIRL: "I want a girl who will be as devoted to me as I will be to her."

PET PEEVE: Rainy days

WHERE TO WRITE TO RICKY: Ricky Schroder
c/o The William Morris Agency
151 El Camino Drive
Beverly Hills, CA 90212

JOHN STAMOS

John Stamos has changed a great deal since his days as Blackie Parrish on *General Hospital*. In the years since he left the soap, he has gone on to star in three prime-time series, *Dreams*, *You Again?* and *Full House*.

Concerned with his career as an actor, John wants to be able to achieve success in every aspect of the business. "I've worked on drama and music and now I'm working hard on comedy," he says. "I want to be able to do everything."

John Phillip Stamotopoulos was born under a golden California Sun on August 19, 1963. He grew up in a close-knit family which includes parents Bill and Loretta, and sisters Janeen and Alaina. Although he gained popularity fast, John feels his family has kept his life in perspective. "They were always there for me," he says proudly.

As a teenager, John liked to goof off. His early years were spent at the beach with his buddies, but he soon felt he was wasting too much time. He knew that if he wanted to be an actor he had to get moving.

After only a few auditions, he landed the role on *General Hospital* which ultimately turned him into a star. But John wasn't satisfied. He became interested in music and formed his own rock band. He sang, played drums and toured the states for two years after leaving *General Hospital*. Still involved in music today, John built his own recording studio in his home and dreams of releasing an album of his own music someday.

When he is asked where he would like to be in ten years, John responds, "I don't really think about it, but I'd like to be thought of as a good actor and a good person with good morals." That is the perfect description of John Stamos today!

JOHN STAMOS' VITAL STATISTICS

FULL REAL NAME: John Phillip Stamotopoulos

BIRTHDATE: August 19, 1963

BIRTHPLACE: Cypress, California

HEIGHT: 5'11"

WEIGHT: 160 lbs.

HAIR: Brown

EYES: Hazel

FAMILY: Dad, Bill; mom, Loretta; sisters, Janeen and Alaina

TELEVISION: *General Hospital, Dreams, You Again?, Full House*

MOVIE: *Never Too Young To Die*

FAVORITE MOVIE: *The Wizard of Oz*

FAVORITE FOOD: Hamburgers, chicken

FAVORITE DESSERT: Ice cream

FAVORITE COLOR: Blue

FAVORITE CITY: New York

FAVORITE BANDS: The Beatles, The Beach Boys

FAVORITE CAR: 1969 blue Mustang convertible, which he owns

FAVORITE SPORTS: Softball and bicycle riding with friends

BEST FRIEND: Kin Shriner, who was on *General Hospital* with him

FAVORITE PASTIMES: Riding all the rides in Disneyland and going to see all the latest movies

WHAT JOHN WOULD'VE DONE IF HE DIDN'T BECOME AN ACTOR: He admits he might have become a dentist

FUTURE GOALS: To keep acting on TV and in the movies

WORST HABIT: Ever the drummer, John is always pounding on things!

WHERE TO WRITE TO JOHN: John Stamos
c/o Jo-Ann Geffen & Associates
3151 Cahuenga Blvd. West
Suite 235
Los Angeles, CA 90028

SCOTT VALENTINE

Playing Nick Moore, Mallory's punky, street-wise, artist boyfriend on *Family Ties* has turned Scott Valentine into a star. After his long and hard road to success, Scott is glad he's been given the chance.

He was born and raised in Saratoga Springs, New York and first discovered acting at age five. "I can remember doing plays in my parents' garage," he says. He appeared in a few high school plays, but didn't pursue acting as a career until his second semester of college. He moved to New York City and studied at the American Academy of Dramatic Arts, where he completed the school's three-year program in a year and a half.

He held a few odd jobs such as short order cook and researcher for a publishing firm, and he won a few roles off-off Broadway. Everything seemed to be going great for Scott. He signed a contract for a daytime soap and was about to screen test for a role in the feature film *Lords of Discipline*. But on the afternoon of September 17, 1981, Scott was accidentally hit by a truck while riding his bicycle through a busy Manhattan street.

Convalescence took almost three years, and then Scott found it difficult to land roles in New York's theatre circuit because he had an artificial hip. Known as "the guy with the limp," he decided to pack his bags and start fresh in Los Angeles.

It wasn't long after his move that he landed his role on *Family Ties*. He has starred in the feature films *My Demon Lover* and *Remembrances from the Garden of Laura*, and there's talk of a spin-off of his character on *Family Ties*. Now in demand, Scott, who has one son, Trevin, with his wife, actress Kym Fischer, feels very fortunate. He says he's always lived by one motto — "Don't give up on your dreams!"

SCOTT VALENTINE'S VITAL STATISTICS

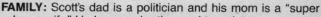

FULL REAL NAME: Scott Eugene Valentine

BIRTHDATE: June 3, 1958

BIRTHPLACE: Saratoga Springs, New York

HEIGHT: 5'11"

WEIGHT: 150 lbs.

HAIR: Brown

EYES: Brown

FAMILY: Scott's dad is a politician and his mom is a "super housewife." He has one brother and two sisters.

MARITAL STATUS: He and his wife, actress Kym Fischer, have one son, Trevin

HOBBIES: Writing, carpentry

FAVORITE SPORTS: Jogging, weightlifting and swimming

FAVORITE BOOKS: He loves reading biographies

FAVORITE MUSICIANS: Jazz great Chick Corea, The Pretenders

TELEVISION: *Family Ties.* He also filmed the pilot for a spin-off called *The Art of Being Nick*

FILMS: *My Demon Lover, Remembrances from the Garden of Laura*

BEST TIME OF HIS LIFE: Getting married. The reception was at a foreign car dealership and the honeymoon was in Acapulco.

WORST TIME OF HIS LIFE: In 1981, he was hit by a truck in Manhattan which shattered his hip and left him unable to work for three years.

FUTURE GOALS: "I'd like to do more movies. I'd also like to get into producing."

WHERE TO WRITE TO SCOTT: Scott Valentine
c/o NBC-TV
3000 West Alameda Ave.
Burbank, CA 91523

JONATHAN WARD

Jonathan Ward has spent half of his life as a professional actor. A small role as an orphan in a dinner theatre production of *Oliver* convinced the young go-getter to make performing his career.

Jonathan William Ward was born on February 24, 1970 to John and Billye Ward. In 1980, at the age of ten, he starred opposite Sandy Duncan in the Broadway revival of *Peter Pan* and followed that with a string of stage performances.

When he moved to California with his family, Jonathan won roles in the television movies *The Haunted Mansion*, *Maid in America*, *Just Another Stupid Kid* and *Orphans, Waifs and Wards*. He made his motion picture debut in *White Water Summer* opposite Kevin Bacon and Sean Astin and appeared in the TV series *Charles in Charge* and *Heart of the City*.

Now starring in *The New Adventures of Beans Baxter*, blue-eyed Jonathan feels how he won the title role was ironic. "We found out *Heart of the City* was canceled and Friday would be our last day of shooting," he explains. "On Thursday, I was riding my bike by the Fox Broadcasting Studios and ran into Savage Steve Holland. He's the executive producer-writer-director for *Beans Baxter*. He told me he thought I was right for the part and I auditioned and got it. I finished taping *Heart of the City* on Friday and started *Beans* on Monday morning."

Offscreen, the light-brown-haired actor likes to scuba dive, sketch and date. He is also the national youth spokesperson for the Adam Walsh Foundation, which is dedicated to finding missing children.

JONATHAN WARD'S VITAL STATISTICS

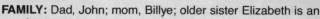

FULL REAL NAME: Jonathan William Ward

BIRTHDATE: February 24, 1970

BIRTHPLACE: Maryland

HEIGHT: 5'8"

WEIGHT: 130 lbs.

HAIR: Light brown

EYES: Pale blue

FAMILY: Dad, John; mom, Billye; older sister Elizabeth is an actress

PET: Dog named Seymour

FAVORITE ROCKERS: Dire Straits

FAVORITE MUSIC: Rock 'n' roll and jazz ·

FAVORITE CLOTHES: Old torn jeans. "I will never buy a pair of new jeans," he says.

FAVORITE SNACK: Popcorn

IDEAL GIRL: "I like honest girls who can carry on a good conversation."

IDEA OF A FUN DATE: "I usually follow the classic date by first going somewhere nice for dinner. I like to take a girl to dinner because that gives us a chance to talk. Afterwards, I like going to the movies or the beach."

THE MOST ROMANTIC THING YOU'VE EVER DONE: "Sometimes I'll go all out and send a girl roses. I like to open doors and pull out chairs for girls, too."

THEATRE CREDIT: Seven years ago, Jonathan starred on Broadway in the play *Peter Pan*

MOVIES: *Whitewater Summer, Mac and Me*

TV SERIES: *Charles in Charge, Heart of the City, The New Adventures of Beans Baxter*

FUTURE GOALS: "My ideal fun role is to play a bad guy," he says smiling. "I'm always playing the all-American kid."

WHERE TO WRITE TO JONATHAN: Jonathan Ward
c/o Fox Broadcasting Television
10201 West Pico Blvd.,
Century City, CA 90035

MALCOLM-JAMAL WARNER

As Theodore Huxtable on *The Cosby Show*, Malcolm-Jamal Warner gets the chance to play the super-hip son of Dr. Huxtable, played by Bill Cosby. Malcolm feels very fortunate to have been chosen for the role because he says he's always "worshipped anything with Bill Cosby in it!"

Born on August 18, 1970 in Jersey City, New Jersey, Malcolm began acting in community theatre in Los Angeles at the age of nine. At thirteen, his agent heard about a casting call for *The Cosby Show*. "They were looking for a six-foot-two-inch fifteen-year-old," says Malcolm. "So at first I wasn't going to go to the audition because I was five-foot, five inches and thirteen. But I went and because they couldn't find anyone to fit the category, they started considering others."

Now, after four years of playing Theo, Malcolm thinks his character is "a cool person." He says if he were to change one thing about Theo it would be "to make him more mature. Although he's funny and smart, Theo believes in taking the easy way out. I think that everything can have a solution if you work at it. I use my brain all the time."

When he has some time for himself, Malcolm can be found playing basketball or listening to music by Janet Jackson, Run D.M.C. and Five Star. "I actually listen to everything except country and heavy metal," he confides.

Despite his success on television, brown-eyed Malcolm says fame hasn't changed him at all. "I'm not affected by it," he assures. "I do everything a normal teenager does. I go out dancing. I go to the movies and love playing basketball with my friends. I'm not any different from anyone else. *The Cosby Show* is my nine-to-five job!"

MALCOLM-JAMAL WARNER'S VITAL STATISTICS

FULL REAL NAME: Malcolm-Jamal Warner

NICKNAME: Mal-Jam

BIRTHDATE: August 18, 1970

BIRTHPLACE: Jersey City, New Jersey

HEIGHT: 5'10"

WEIGHT: 140 lbs.

HAIR: Black

EYES: Brown

FAMILY: Dad, Robert; mom, Pamela; one older half-brother and one older half-sister

FIRST AMBITION: "My dream was to play basketball for the Los Angeles Lakers with my idol, Kareem Abdul-Jabbar."

FIRST JOB: Bag boy at a grocery store

FAVORITE MUSICIANS: Run D.M.C., Five Star, Janet Jackson

FAVORITE SPORTS: Basketball, football, track

HOBBIES: Dancing, hanging out with friends

MOST EMBARRASSING MOMENT: Being on TV's *Bloopers and Practical Jokes*

PET PEEVE: Phony, insensitive people

SELF-DESCRIPTION: Understanding

FAVORITE QUOTE: "Hard work is the key to success."

HIS FEELINGS ON HIS CHARACTER, THEODORE: "I like being the only boy on *The Cosby Show*. Being in the minority gives you the opportunity to stand out."

FUTURE GOALS: "If I ever come to realize that acting isn't what I want to do with my life, I think I'd like to go into computers or law — or both!"

FANTASY: To ride on a flying unicorn into the future

WHERE TO WRITE TO MALCOLM-JAMAL: Malcolm-Jamal Warner
c/o NBC-TV
3000 West Alameda Avenue
Burbank, CA 91523

TINA YOTHERS

Tina Yothers began doing commercials when she was just three years old. The daughter of TV film producer Robert Yothers, she was born on May 5, 1973 in Whittier, California. Her three brothers had all acted in commercials and Tina says she was "brought up in dressing rooms."

After doing spots for McDonalds, Bell Telephone and Doritos, Tina auditioned for a role in the movie *Shoot The Moon* and won the part. "I got the first (role) I tried out for," says Tina. "Right after *Shoot The Moon*, I got *Family Ties*. The star of the movie was Diane Keaton and the producer of *Family Ties* loves her. That's why the family name on the show is Keaton."

Having played the role of Jennifer Keaton since she was eight years old, Tina finds she can relate to her character. "In a very big way it's me playing Jennifer," she confides. "I know her almost as well as I know myself."

In her spare time, green-eyed Tina enjoys playing sports, especially swimming and hockey. "My brothers all play hockey," she notes. "So that's my favorite sport." Her favorite singers are Shirley Jones and Howard Hewitt and she says she would like to visit Moscow again because she had such a great time there.

Tina plans on staying with *Family Ties* for as long as it stays on the air. "We're like one big happy family," she boasts of the cast. Recently, this talented actress wrote a book called *Being Your Best: Tina Yothers' Guide for Girls* and appeared in a TV movie, *Crash Course*. Her manager dad is also producing her first album.

TINA YOTHERS' VITAL STATISTICS

FULL REAL NAME: Tina Yothers
BIRTHDATE: May 5, 1973
BIRTHPLACE: Whittier, California
HEIGHT: 5'3"
WEIGHT: 110 lbs.
HAIR: Blonde
EYES: Blue
FAMILY: Parents, sister and three brothers, Jeff, Randy and Corey.
CURRENT RESIDENCE: Roland Heights, California
FIRST ACTING BREAK: She started doing commercials at age three.
TV ROLE: Jennifer Keaton on *Family Ties*
MOVIE: *Shoot the Moon*
TV MOVIE: *Crash Course*
FAVORITE SINGERS: Howard Hewitt, Shirley Jones
FAVORITE SPORTS: Swimming, hockey
FAVORITE WAY TO SPEND FREE TIME: "I work with organizations helping people."
FAVORITE FOOD: Junk food. "I like to have a Big Mac once in a while," she admits.
FAVORITE PLACE TO VISIT: "I'd like to go back to Moscow. I went there last year for four days and had a great time."
BEST FRIEND ON THE SET OF *FAMILY TIES:* Michael Gross, who plays her father, Steven Keaton. "A lot of kids out there would like to have a father like Michael."
HOW SHE RELATES TO HER CHARACTER ON *FAMILY TIES:* "In a big way, it's me playing Jennifer. I don't think any actor or actress can ever play a totally different role without including a little of themselves."
OTHER ACHIEVEMENTS: Tina wrote a book called *Being Your Best: Tina Yothers' Guide for Girls*.
WHERE TO WRITE TO TINA: Tina Yothers
c/o NBC-TV
3000 W. Alameda Ave.
Burbank, CA 91523

PART TWO
MOVIE STARS

SEAN ASTIN

Of all the movies Sean Astin has starred in, his favorites are the comedies. "It's great to make people laugh," he says and he hopes to continue starring in movies like his most recent, *Like Father, Like Son* with Kirk Cameron.

Sean Patrick Astin was born on February 25, 1971 to actress Patty Duke and actor John Astin. When he was very young, he wanted to be a policeman and a fireman, but says, "As soon as I was able to comprehend what my parents did, that's all I wanted to do." At the age of eight, he appeared opposite his mother in *Please Don't Hit Me Mom* and soon after made his feature film debut as Mikey Walsh in *The Goonies*.

"I had the best time on that set," he remembers. "I learned so much about making movies, about acting and how special effects are done." He followed that with the Disney TV movie *B.R.A.T. Patrol* and also starred in *White Water Summer* opposite Kevin Bacon.

In *Like Father, Like Son,* Sean plays Trigger, Kirk Cameron's best friend. Sean says, "I had only met Kirk once and when I was cast in this movie, everyone told me what a nice guy he was. I became good friends with him and the set was real comfortable."

When Sean finds time for himself, he likes riding his bicycle around the streets of Westwood, California. His favorite music is classical and he is an old movie buff. One thing he knows is that he always wants to be acting. His next movie is called *A Boy's Life*.

"I'm happy with the way things are right now," smiles Sean. "I like the direction my life is going in and hope it will continue like this in the future."

SEAN ASTIN'S VITAL STATISTICS

FULL REAL NAME: Sean Patrick Astin

BIRTHDATE: February 25, 1971

BIRTHPLACE: Los Angeles, California

HEIGHT: 5'5"

WEIGHT: 125 lbs.

HAIR: Sandy blond

EYES: Green

FAMILY: Mom, Patty Duke Pearce; dad, John Astin; brothers, Mackenzie, David, Allen and Tom

PETS: Two dogs, Kismet and Pappy, one turtle and one snake

FAVORITE SINGERS: Billy Joel, Cyndi Lauper

FAVORITE MOVIE: *Casablanca*

FAVORITE COLOR: Blue

FAVORITE FOODS: "All-American hamburgers, lobster, dad's blintzes and mom's sloppy Joes."

FAVORITE PASTIME: "Every sport you can imagine!"

FAVORITE CLOTHES: "Anything comfortable. One thing I've never been is clothes-conscious."

WHAT KIND OF GIRL DOES SEAN LIKE?: "I like all girls, as long as they are nice," he smiles.

HOW WOULD SEAN DESCRIBE HIMSELF?: "Honest and outgoing!"

BEST ADVICE HE'S EVER RECEIVED: "When I first told my parents I wanted to act, they said, 'Don't push it. Let everything come one step at a time.'"

MOVIES: *The Goonies, B.R.A.T. Patrol, White Water Summer, Like Father, Like Son, A Boy's Life*

WHERE TO MEET SEAN: He loves going to baseball games with brother Mackenzie, as well as movies and rock concerts.

WHERE TO WRITE TO SEAN: Sean Astin
c/o Contemporary-Korman
Artists, Ltd.
132 Lasky Drive
Beverly Hills, CA 90212

KEVIN BACON

The role which brought blue-eyed Kevin Bacon to prominence was Fenwick in the hit film *Diner*. Before that, he had enjoyed success on Broadway, where he learned a lot about his craft.

Kevin, who was born and raised in Philadelphia, Pennsylvania, says, "Having five older brothers and sisters, I had a need to perform." He began taking drama lessons at age thirteen and went on to become the youngest member of the Manning Street Actor's Theatre in Philadelphia.

At age eighteen, he left home to pursue his acting dreams further and quickly gained attention on the New York stage. He made his Broadway debut in *Slab Boys* opposite Sean Penn and won a role in the television movie *Mister Roberts*.

Kevin has had major roles in *Friday the 13th*, *Animal House*, *Hero At Large*, *Only When I Laugh* and *Diner*. With his terrific screen presence, confidence and charm, it didn't take him long to also star in his own vehicles, *Footloose*, *Quicksilver*, *White Water Summer* and, most recently, *She's Having A Baby*.

Kevin finds acting very fullfilling and works hard at being the best he can be. But despite his success, he has remained as humble as the first day he began his career. "That's not to say I don't want to be rich and famous like everyone else," he laughs, with a twinkle in his eye. "But it's more important for me to do good work. I want to be a good actor, not a star."

When he isn't working, Kevin unwinds in his Connecticut farmhouse. His longtime girlfriend Tracy Pollan left him for Michael J. Fox, but Kevin has since found romance with actress Kyra Sedgwick. Though his career is a primary concern, Kevin confides, "My family, friends and my health are the most important parts of my life!"

KEVIN BACON'S VITAL STATISTICS

FULL REAL NAME: Kevin Bacon

BIRTHDATE: July 8, 1958

BIRTHPLACE: Philadelphia, Pa.

HEIGHT: 5'10"

WEIGHT: 160 lbs.

HAIR: Blond

EYES: Blue

FAMILY: His parents still live in Pennsylvania. Kevin has five older brothers and sisters.

FILMS: *Friday the 13th, Animal House, Hero At Large, Only When I Laugh, Diner, Footloose, Quicksilver, White Water Summer, She's Having A Baby*

TELEVISION: *The Guiding Light*

TV MOVIE: *Mister Roberts*

BIGGEST THRILL: At age sixteen, he and a friend went on a back-packing journey from Pennsylvania to California and back again.

CURRENT RESIDENCE: He has his own apartment in New York City

SECRET GETAWAY: His farmhouse in Connecticut on twenty-two acres.

LITTLE KNOWN FACT: Kevin is also a singer/songwriter and a jazz and ballet dancer

FAVORITE PASTIMES: Cooking gourmet meals, riding his horse and gardening

FAVORITE EXPERIENCE AS AN ACTOR: Working in theatre. "I feel if I do a play every year, and some readings, it's satisfying in a way cinema is not."

FUTURE GOALS: "My goal is not to be a star, but to be a good actor."

WHERE TO WRITE TO KEVIN: Kevin Bacon
c/o Heidi Schaeffer
8436 West 3rd Street
Los Angeles, CA 90048

MATTHEW BRODERICK

Dubbed "the toast of two coasts" by the *Los Angeles Times*, Matthew Broderick has charmed audiences both on Broadway and the silver screen. Born and raised in Manhattan, Matthew grew up surrounded by theatre. The first bit of acting he did was in a school production of *A Midsummer Night's Dream*. "I felt very confident," Matthew says now. "I even impressed myself."

Shortly before graduation from New York's Walden School, he made his professional acting debut off-Broadway opposite his father, the late actor James Broderick, in the Horton Foote play *Valentine's Day*. That experience made him realize he wanted to pursue acting as a career. He began studying with drama teacher Uta Hagen and voice coach Robert Leonard, but credits his parents with being the major forces in his career.

Matthew's performance in *Torch Song Trilogy* won him an Outer Circle Award as well as the Villager Award and rave reviews from the critics. He also caught the eye of playwright Neil Simon who cast him not only as Eugene Morris Jerome in *Brighton Beach Memoirs*, but also as Marsha Mason's son in his first movie, *Max Dugan Returns*.

When he won the Tony Award for *Brighton Beach Memoirs*, Matthew proudly dedicated it to his father. James Broderick had died of cancer shortly before Matthew began rehearsals for the play.

The bright new star appeared in such successful films as *WarGames*, *Ladyhawke*, *Ferris Bueller's Day Off* and *Project X*. He got the chance to reprise his role of Eugene on Broadway in *Biloxi Blues* and is presently starring in the movie version of the play.

MATTHEW BRODERICK'S VITAL STATISTICS

FULL REAL NAME: Matthew Broderick

NICKNAME: As a child, it was Monkey. Now it's Matty.

BIRTHDATE: March 21, 1962

BIRTHPLACE: New York, New York

HAIR: Brown

EYES: Brown

FAMILY: Mom, Patricia; sisters, Martha and Janet. His father was actor James Broderick, who died the night Matthew began rehearsing for *Brighton Beach Memoirs*

GIRLFRIEND: Jennifer Grey

HIGH SCHOOL ATTENDED: Matthew attended the Walden School, a small private school in New York City

FIRST ACTING BREAK: The H.B. Studio production of *Valentine's Day* co-starring his father

STAGE CREDITS: *Torch Song Trilogy*, *Brighton Beach Memoirs*, *Biloxi Blues*

FILMS: *WarGames*, *Ladyhawke*, *Max Dugan Returns*, *1918*, *Ferris Bueller's Day Off*, *Project X* and *Biloxi Blues*

TELEVISION: *Master Harold and the Boys*

BIGGEST THRILL: Winning the Tony Award for his role in *Brighton Beach Memoirs*

HOBBIES: Rollerskating, astronomy, reading

FAVORITE ACTOR: Jackie Gleason

FAVORITE FOOD: Italian, Big Macs

FAVORITE DESSERT: Ice cream

FAVORITE GAME: Monopoly

SELF-DESCRIPTION: "I'm shy when I first meet someone. It takes me a while to warm up to people. But after I get to know a person, I don't think I'm shy."

WHERE TO WRITE TO MATTHEW: Matthew Broderick
151 El Camino Drive
Beverly Hills, CA 90212

TOM CRUISE

Talented Tom Cruise first fell in love with acting when he auditioned for the lead role of Nathan Detroit in a high school production of *Guys and Dolls* and won it. From his first performance, Tom knew he wanted to become a professional.

Thomas Cruise Mapother IV was born in Syracuse, New York on July 3, 1962 to Marylee and Thomas Cruise Mapother III. Because of his father's job as an electrical engineer, his childhood was spent traveling from one city to the next. When he was eleven, his parents divorced and five years later, his mother remarried. Marylee and her second husband, Jack, moved Tom and his three sisters to Glen Ridge, New Jersey.

After graduating from high school, the future actor set out for New York and started auditioning. Within five months of waiting tables and pounding the pavement, he landed a small role in the feature film *Endless Love*. Through his drive and ambition, he was cast in *Taps*, *Losin' It* and *The Outsiders*.

His extraordinary screen presence was evident right from the start and handsome Tom was soon starring in his own films, *Risky Business*, *All the Right Moves* and *Legend*. *Legend*, a fantasy-adventure, was filmed in London. Just before Tom left to begin shooting it, his father died of cancer.

Plunging into his work, Tom filmed *Legend* and *Top Gun* back-to-back and followed them with *The Color of Money*, in which he starred opposite Paul Newman, and *Cocktail*. In his latest film, *The Rainman*, he stars with Dustin Hoffman.

In May 1987, he married his longtime sweetheart Mimi Rogers and the couple bought their dream house in Connecticut. The serious-minded actor has already been honored with a star on the Hollywood Walk of Fame and plans to remain an actor all his life.

TOM CRUISE'S VITAL STATISTICS

FULL REAL NAME: Thomas Cruise Mapother IV

BIRTHDATE: July 3, 1962

BIRTHPLACE: Syracuse, New York

HEIGHT: 5′9″

WEIGHT: 150 lbs.

HAIR: Brown

EYES: Blue

FAMILY: Mom, Marylee; sisters, Lee Anne, Marian and Cass. Tom's father, Thomas Cruise Mapother III, died of cancer right before Tom began filming *Legend*

MARITAL STATUS: Married to actress Mimi Rogers

BEST FRIEND: Emilio Estevez

FIRST AMBITIONS: He originally wanted to go into sports, but a knee injury ended that dream. Before pursuing an acting career, Tom studied to be a Franciscan priest. He gave it up after one year because "I realized I loved women too much."

LITTLE KNOWN FACT: Tom, his mother and sisters all have a reading disorder, dyslexia

FILMS: *Endless Love, Taps, Losin' It, Risky Business, All the Right Moves, Legend, Top Gun, The Color of Money, Rainman, Cocktail*

BIGGEST THRILL: Receiving his own star on the Hollywood Walk of Fame

WHAT HE LIKES BEST ABOUT ACTING: "Acting has helped me mature."

FAVORITE ACTOR: Robert DeNiro

FAVORITE MUSICIAN: Vangelis

FAVORITE SPORT: Running

SELF-DESCRIPTION: "I'm sort of a loner and people know many different sides of me. But probably not too many people know me completely."

WHERE TO WRITE TO TOM: Tom Cruise
4708 Vesper Avenue
Sherman Oaks, CA 91403

JON CRYER

Comedy has always played an important part in Jon Cryer's life. The son of actors David and Gretchen Cryer, he always strove for a career in show business.

"I was the class clown in school," says Jon, who attended the Bronx High School of Science. "I used humor to make friends and it was a fun role to play."

Jon's early training included four summers at the Stagedoor Manor Performing Arts Training Center in the Berkshires. In his final year, he was awarded the Center's Best Actor Award. His big break came when he understudied Matthew Broderick in *Brighton Beach Memoirs* and later took over the role.

He made his silver screen debut in the movie *O.C. and Stiggs*, but his real breakthrough was in the teen-oriented film *No Small Affair*.

He says he loved playing Duckie Dale in the smash hit movie *Pretty in Pink*. Of his role, Jon notes, "Duckie was a special kind of guy who I understood very well by the end of shooting." As the king of the zoids, Duckie has an eight-year crush on Andie Walsh, played by Molly Ringwald.

"Molly and I had no kissing scenes in *Pretty in Pink*," Jon begins with a grin. "I think it was because I have lips the size of Las Vegas and they were scared that if I kissed Molly, our lips would stick together," he remarks, laughing.

Jon Cryer's likeable down-to-earth charm has caught the eye of many producers. As the star of three recent movies, *Dudes*, *Superman IV* and *Hiding Out*, the once-shy actor is on the verge of taking Hollywood by storm.

JON CRYER'S VITAL STATISTICS

FULL REAL NAME: Jonathan Niven Cryer

BIRTHDATE: April 16, 1965

BIRTHPLACE: New York City

HEIGHT: 5'9"

WEIGHT: 140 lbs.

HAIR: Dark brown

EYES: Brown

FAMILY: Dad, actor David; mom, actress Gretchen; two sisters

FIRST ACTING JOBS: On stage in Los Angeles in *Torch Song Trilogy*; in New York in *Brighton Beach Memoirs*

SCHOOL ATTENDED: Jon graduated from the Bronx High School of Science

FILMS: *No Small Affair, O.C. & Stiggs, Pretty in Pink, Morgan Stewart's Coming Home, Superman IV, Dudes, Hiding Out*

IDEAL GIRL: Someone he can talk to about acting and who likes doing offbeat things.

FAVORITE COLOR: Black

ROLE THAT'S CLOSEST TO HIS REAL LIFE SELF: "I am most like Duckie in *Pretty in Pink*. It was fun playing him because I always felt like a zoid in high school."

WATCHING HIMSELF ON SCREEN: "Everytime I see myself on screen, I vow never to do it again."

FAVORITE BANDS: INXS, Big Audio Dynamite, Midnight Oil

FUTURE GOALS: He's writing a screenplay and hopes to direct one day.

WHERE TO WRITE TO JON: Jon Cryer
c/o Martin Tudor Productions
125 West 3rd Street
New York, NY 10012

MATT DILLON

Playing rebels in the movies has been Matt Dillon's claim to fame. With roles in such "troubled teenage movies" as *Over the Edge*, *Tex*, *The Outsiders*, *Rumble Fish* and *My Bodyguard*, this hazel-eyed heartthrob almost became an overnight sensation.

Matthew Raymond Dillon was "discovered" while cutting classes in junior high school and quickly went from being a student in Larchmont, New York to one of the most sought-after young actors in Hollywood. His dark good looks certainly have a lot to do with Matt's popularity, but as he progressed from one film to the next, it was evident how talented he really was. Still, it wasn't until he starred in *The Flamingo Kid* that he was really taken seriously.

Although he played a teenager, his performance was a sensitive study of a boy who learns about life and love when he gets a summer job at the El Flamingo, a posh beach club in Rockaway. Matt described his role of Jeffrey Willis as "a guy who gets dazzled by the flash and trash."

The success of *The Flamingo Kid* led Matt to star in *Target*, *Rebel* and *Native Son*. His newest films, *The Big Town* and *Kansas*, prove that he is one actor who can tackle any role successfully.

When Matt isn't thinking about work, he loves going to rock and roll clubs and dating pretty girls. For quiet times, Matt, who lives in New York City's SoHo district, likes to catch up on his reading. As for his future in acting, he says, "It's very important to me and I want to know that I could be the best at it."

MATT DILLON'S VITAL STATISTICS

FULL REAL NAME: Matthew Raymond Dillon

BIRTHDATE: February 18, 1964

BIRTHPLACE: Larchmont, New York

HEIGHT: 5'11"

WEIGHT: 160 lbs.

HAIR: Brown

EYES: Hazel

FAMILY: Dad, Paul; mom, Mary Ellen; brothers, Kevin, Paul, Jr., Tim, Brian; sister, Kate

FIRST AMBITION: To be a lumberjack

FILMS: *Over The Edge, Little Darlings, My Bodyguard, Liar's Moon, Tex, The Outsiders, Rumble Fish, The Flamingo Kid, Target, Rebel, Native Son, Kansas, The Big Town*

HOBBIES: Astrology, reading

FAVORITE COLOR: Black

FAVORITE FOOD: Italian

FAVORITE SPORT: Football

FAVORITE ACTOR: Robert DeNiro

IDEAL GIRL: Someone who is intelligent, understanding and loyal.

PLACE HE'D LOVE TO VISIT: Moscow

CURRENT RESIDENCE: Matt lives in his own apartment in New York City's SoHo area

CAR: Porsche 924

FAVORITE CLUBS: New York's Hard Rock Cafe, The Limelight (also in Manhattan)

SELF-DESCRIPTION: "I'm just a regular American kid."

WHERE TO WRITE TO MATT: Matt Dillon
P.O. Box 800
Old Chelsea Station
New York, NY 10011

EMILIO ESTEVEZ

Acting isn't the only career on Emilio Estevez's mind. He made his debut as a screenwriter by adapting the S.E. Hinton novel *That Was Then, This Is Now* into a major motion picture and wrote and directed the film *Wisdom*. "It wasn't ego that made me do it," he insists. "I just felt that I had the energy to do all three jobs."

Born in Manhattan and raised in Los Angeles, the son of actor Martin Sheen has been dabbling in movie-making his whole life. "I used to make little eight milli-meter films," says Emilio. "I'd edit them and I'd be the cinematographer and the director. Often, I'd be in them, so this was a natural progression for me."

On the day he graduated from Santa Monica High School, Emilio landed his first acting job in an After-school Special, *Seventeen Going on Nowhere*. He was also featured in the TV movies *To Climb A Mountain* and the critically acclaimed *In the Custody of Strangers*. His first movie role was as Matt Dillon's friend in *Tex* and he fol-lowed that up with roles in *The Outsiders*, *Repo Man*, *The Breakfast Club*, *Wisdom* and *Maximum Overdrive*. Emilio has emerged as one of the best young actors around to-day. His accepting a list of challenging roles has had a lot to do with his success. It is obvious that Emilio has grown up on film and his recent movie, *Stakeout*, proves his talents and longevity as a full-fledged star.

Though Emilio wants to be accepted as a serious actor, he isn't ruling out experimenting with his craft. "We all crave those juicy, dramatic roles," he allows. "But it's important to mix and match in a career." And that's just what he intends to do.

EMILIO ESTEVEZ'S VITAL STATISTICS

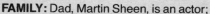

FULL REAL NAME: Emilio Estevez
BIRTHDATE: May 12, 1962
BIRTHPLACE: New York City
HEIGHT: 5'8"
WEIGHT: 140 lbs.
HAIR: Blond
EYES: Blue
FAMILY: Dad, Martin Sheen, is an actor; mom, Janet, is a film producer; brothers Charlie, Ramon and sister Renee are all actors
FAVORITE ACTORS: His dad, James Dean, Robert DeNiro
FAVORITE SINGER: Bruce Springsteen
FAVORITE TV SHOW: *Miami Vice*
FAVORITE SPORT: Working out
FAVORITE FOOD: "Whatever's in the fridge!"
FILMS: *Tex, The Outsiders, Repo Man, The Breakfast Club, St. Elmo's Fire, That Was Then, This Is Now, Maximum Overdrive, Wisdom, Stakeout*
MARITAL STATUS: Single
GIRLFRIEND: After he split from longtime girlfriend Demi Moore, he began dating The Bangles' Susanna Hoffs
WHAT HE LIKES BEST ABOUT ACTING: "Acting gives you the license to be crazy. By that I mean I can portray a range of characters. I can be a doctor, a hoodlum, an athlete or whatever. The possibilities are endless. If I tried doing that in real life, they'd lock me up."
SELF-DESCRIPTION: "I'm extremely disciplined. I like to be alone so I can write and be productive."
WHERE TO WRITE TO EMILIO: Emilio Estevez
c/o CAA
1888 Century Park East, Suite 1400
Los Angeles, CA 90067

COREY FELDMAN

Corey Feldman isn't the kind of guy who is egotistical about fame. "The thing that really bothers me," he says, "is someone who is stuck up because he's been lucky to get a part in a movie."

Corey was born on July 16, 1971, and his mom and dad put him into the business at the age of three. His first big break was a commercial for McDonald's Gift Certificates, which still runs every Christmas. Since then he has appeared in over one hundred commercials and guest-starred on fifty TV shows.

His debut in the feature film *Gremlins* was followed by *The Goonies* and Corey felt fortunate to be part of both films. "I got to work with Steven Spielberg on my first two movies and he is a really nice guy," he says. "The most fun I've had on a movie had to be on *The Goonies* because I experienced things I've never experienced before."

After lending his acting talents to *Friday the 13th* (Parts 4 and 5), Corey starred in his favorite movie to date, *Stand By Me*. He said of his performance as Teddy in that film, "Usually I cringe when I see myself in movies. But *Stand By Me* was the first time I thought I was good." In *The Lost Boys*, Corey played a different kind of part. "I play this junior Rambo character," he notes. "It was a lot of fun because he's so different from the way I really am."

When Corey is away from the cameras, he's not at all like the wild guy he plays onscreen. "I'm shy and sensitive," he offers. In the future, he thinks he would like to go into music, but is dedicated to acting. "I know I'll be an actor all my life," he says with assurance.

COREY FELDMAN'S VITAL STATISTICS

FULL REAL NAME: Corey Scott Feldman

NICKNAME: Core

BIRTHDATE: July 16, 1971

BIRTHPLACE: Encino, California

HEIGHT: 5'7"

WEIGHT: 120 lbs.

HAIR: Dark blond

EYES: Brown

FAMILY: Dad, Bob; mom, Sheila; sisters, Eden, Mindy; brother, Devin

FAVORITE CHILDHOOD MEMORY: "My first girlfriend!"

FAVORITE FOOD: Pizza, spaghetti

FAVORITE DESSERT: Ice cream

FAVORITE SINGER: Michael Jackson

FIRST ACTING BREAK: "I started doing commercials when I was three years old. My first big one was for McDonalds Gift Certificates.

FILMS: *Gremlins*, *Goonies*, *Friday the 13th* (Parts 4 and 5), *Stand By Me*, *The Lost Boys*, *License to Drive*.

IDEAL GIRL: "Someone who is real honest and has a good sense of humor. I like a girl who is very beautiful on the inside and out."

FEELINGS ON FANS: "I really appreciate it when someone wants my autograph. I'll always take the time to give it no matter where I am or how busy I am."

SELF-DESCRIPTION: "I'm a shy and quiet person. I'm not really a wild guy."

WHERE TO WRITE TO COREY: Corey Feldman
2138 N. Cahuenga Blvd.
Hollywood, CA 90068

ANDRE GOWER

In a few short years, Andre Gower has built up an impressive list of credits. Only fourteen years old, the cute, sandy-blond-haired actor has already starred in four TV movies, three soap operas and the feature films *Summer Heat* and *The Monster Squad*.

He was born Jon Andre Gower on April 27, 1973 and grew up in the San Fernando Valley. When he was seven years old, he began acting. "My sister, Carlena, was in the business before me," he says. "And it's because of her that I got interested in it at all."

Andre won a role in the movie *Summer Heat* and did more than one hundred commercials. He then played Brooks Prentis on the soap opera *The Young and the Restless* for one year and appeared in recurring roles on *Days of Our Lives* and *General Hospital*.

While working on the television show *The Wizard*, he went on an audition for *The Monster Squad*. "I really liked the script," says hazel-eyed Andre. "And I knew I'd like to be in it." He was excited when he won the role and says Sean was a great character to play "because he's determined. When he wants to do something, he doesn't fool around."

Andre, who rarely has time off, also appears as Nick Tresch on the television series *Mr. President*. "I walked onto the set the first day and I felt as if I were on sacred ground," recalls Andre. "I thought, 'This is the White House!'"

When he has some time for himself, this ninety-six pound bundle of energy enjoys basketball, tennis and archery. He also likes to date and says he goes for a girl "who is lively and energetic" — two words which describe Andre perfectly!

ANDRE GOWER'S VITAL STATISTICS

FULL REAL NAME: Jon Andre Gower

BIRTHDATE: April 27, 1973

BIRTHPLACE: Los Angeles, California

HEIGHT: 4'11"

WEIGHT: 96 lbs.

HAIR: Sandy blond

EYES: Hazel

FAMILY: Dad, John; mom, Dorothy; sister, Carlena (18)

PET: Dog named Bit

FIRST RECORD BOUGHT: *Winnie the Pooh*

FAVORITE COLORS: Red, white, black, blue

FAVORITE FOOD: Mexican, Italian

FAVORITE TV SHOWS: *L.A. Law, MacGyver*

FAVORITE SINGER: Billy Joel

FAVORITE MOVIE: *The Monster Squad*

FAVORITE SPORTS: Archery, basketball, tennis

FAVORITE CLOTHES: Dapper and funky

FAVORITE ACTOR: Clint Eastwood

FAVORITE ACTRESS: Jaclyn Smith

IDEA OF A FUN DATE: Expensive and romantic

HOW WOULD ANDRE DESCRIBE HIMSELF?: Determined

BEST FEATURES: "My hands and hair."

WHERE TO WRITE TO ANDRE: Andre Gower
c/o Talent Access
14155 Gilmore Street #5
Van Nuys, CA 91401

COREY HAIM

At the age of eleven, Corey Haim began his acting career appearing in commercials in his native Toronto. A casting agent saw his work and signed him as a regular on the popular Canadian children's show *The Edison Twins*.

His film debut, playing the volatile younger son of Teri Garr in *First Born*, had an immediate impact in Hollywood. Acting came easy for him right from the beginning. "I never did anything to prepare myself for a scene," he says. "I just went in and did it."

Within a twelve-month span, Corey was cast in three movies, *Secret Admirer*, *Silver Bullet* and *Murphy's Romance*. It was while he was filming *Murphy's Romance* in Florence, Arizona that he was cast in his first starring role — in *Lucas*. In the filmmakers' quest for the perfect Lucas, Corey was a last-minute choice. They flew to Arizona to meet with him and his family to talk over the role. Though his mother wanted him to take a break after filming three movies back-to-back, Corey didn't want to miss this chance at a leading role. The day after the filmmakers met him in Arizona, they flew him to Los Angeles for a screen test and he won the role.

Corey is very energetic and finds it difficult to sit still for long. He played Matthew Wiggins on the short-lived TV series *Roomies* and filmed *The Lost Boys* at the same time. When he isn't working in movies, a typical day for Corey is "to go to school, come home and practice my synthesizer!"

Looking ahead to his future, Corey would like to star opposite Sly Stallone in a Rambo-type role because he is tired of playing straight kids and nerds. When it comes to girls, the blue-eyed actor admits, "I'm a terrible boyfriend. I have a lot of growing up to do because I just can't handle going steady yet."

COREY HAIM'S VITAL STATISTICS

FULL REAL NAME: Corey Ian Haim

NICKNAMES: Corky, Corkscrew, Space Ace

BIRTHDATE: December 23, 1971

BIRTHPLACE: Toronto, Canada

HEIGHT: 5'6"

WEIGHT: 120 lbs.

HAIR: Dark blond

EYES: Blue

FAMILY: Parents Bernie and Judy are separated; one sister, Carol

FAVORITE CITY: Los Angeles, California

FAVORITE ACTOR: Sylvester Stallone

FAVORITE COLOR: Blue

FAVORITE FOOD: Pizza

FAVORITE DRINK: Lemonade

FAVORITE CHILDHOOD MEMORY: "Sneaking into my first R-rated movie."

BIGGEST INFLUENCES ON HIS LIFE: "My mom, dad and sister — cause they're my family!"

FILMS: *First Born, Secret Admirer, Silver Bullet, Murphy's Romance, Lucas, The Lost Boys, License to Drive.*

TELEVISION: *The Edison Twins* (Canadian TV show), *Roomies*

TV MOVIE: *A Time To Live*

ONE THING HE LIKES BEST ABOUT HIMSELF: "My nickname Space Ace."

WORST HABIT: "Biting my nails."

BIGGEST FEAR: Sharks

PET PEEVE: Talking on the telephone

WHERE TO WRITE TO COREY: Corey Haim
c/o Baker/Winoky/Ryder
Public Relations
9348 Civic Center Drive
Suite 407
Beverly Hills, CA 90210

C. THOMAS HOWELL

Since his feature film debut in *E.T. The Extra-Terrestrial*, C. Thomas Howell has achieved remarkable success as the star of films *The Outsiders*, *Tank*, *Grandview U.S.A.*, *Red Dawn*, *Secret Admirer*, *The Hitcher*, *Soul Man* and *A Tiger's Tale*.

Tommy, as he likes to be called, was born on December 7, 1966 in Van Nuys, California and never planned on acting as a career. The son of rodeo-riding, stuntman Christopher Howell, Sr., Tommy intended to follow in his father's footsteps. A rider since the age of six, he won the prestigious All Around Cowboy Award by the California Junior Rodeo Association in 1979.

Acting seemed to fall in Tommy's lap and in the beginning he just did it for fun. He began at age five when he appeared in a TV show called *Little People*. Seven years later, he acted opposite Marlo Thomas in *It Happened One Christmas* and in an Afterschool Special, *Thunder*. His love for acting really began to take shape when he was cast as Ponyboy in *The Outsiders*. He spent the next few years filming one movie after another and looks forward to starring in even more challenging roles in the future.

Offscreen, Tommy's favorite hobby remains rodeo riding and for quiet times he enjoys camping. He dates actress Rae Dawn Chong and likes to visit New York City because "there's something to do 24 hours a day."

Tommy's dad is now the stunt coordinator of TV's *Moonlighting* and Tommy did a stunt last season. With so many different things going on in this gorgeous guy's life, he says matter-of-factly, "I like being involved with projects and having responsibilities."

C. THOMAS HOWELL'S VITAL STATISTICS

FULL REAL NAME: Christopher Thomas Howell, Jr.

NICKNAME: Buckwheat

BIRTHDATE: December 7, 1966

BIRTHPLACE: Van Nuys, California

HEIGHT: 5'10"

WEIGHT: 140 lbs.

HAIR: Light brown

EYES: Hazel

FIRST AMBITION: First he wanted to be an architect, then a stuntman like his dad

FAMILY: Dad, Chris; mom, Candace; two younger sisters, Stacy and Candy, younger brother, Jon

FIRST ACTING BREAK: He had a small role in *E.T.*

FILMS: *The Outsiders, Red Dawn, Tank, Secret Admirer, The Hitcher, Soul Man, A Tiger's Tale*

FIRST GIRLFRIEND: A girl named Mia in the first grade. "She was the first girl I ever kissed," he says.

IDEAL GIRL: "Someone who isn't overly impressed with herself and has a good sense of humor"

PET PEEVES: Liars and snobs

WHAT HE LIKES ABOUT HIMSELF: His sense of humor

OTHER ACCOMPLISHMENTS: He was named California Junior Rodeo Association Champion in 1979

FAVORITE SPORTS: Snow and water skiing, horseback riding, football and dirtbike riding

FAVORITE COLORS: Black, red, yellow, white

SCARIEST MOMENT: During the filming of *The Hitcher* when Rutger Hauer held a knife to his eye. "I was so scared," admits Tommy. "I kept thinking, 'What if he slips?'"

WHERE TO WRITE TO TOMMY: C. Thomas Howell
P.O. Box 761
Woodland Hills, CA 91365

RYAN LAMBERT

Ryan Lambert recently wrapped up filming his first movie, *The Monster Squad*. His comments about that experience? "Doing a movie is really cool. Now I want to do films all the time."

Born on March 29, 1971 to Robert and Marlene Lambert, Ryan admits he always dreamed of becoming an actor. He got his first taste of performing in local productions of *Salute to Broadway*, *Christmas Follies* and *George M*. At fourteen, he auditioned for a part on the Disney Channel show *Kids, Inc.* and became a series regular.

In *The Monster Squad*, he plays Rudy Halloran, a character for whom he had a feel from his first reading. "I knew that Rudy was a real tough guy who smokes and drinks. So when I walked in to the reading the first thing I asked for was a cigarette and I just grabbed one from the desk and lit up. I felt I really was Rudy and I guess the casting people did, too!"

Ryan, who doesn't smoke or drink, describes his character as "a 50s greaser type. He dresses like the Fonz, acts like Mickey Rourke and is really cool like James Dean." Then with a grin, he adds, "James Dean is my hero. He's number one — all the way!"

Ryan claims there are many wonderful rewards that go along with his job. "The best part is the fans. When I got my first fan letter, I was so happy, I framed it," he smiles, thinking back.

The next step for Ryan is to take on a more serious role. "I think I am ready to do something like Eric Stoltz did in *Mask*," he says. "I want to be considered a serious actor in the future!"

RYAN LAMBERT'S VITAL STATISTICS

FULL REAL NAME: Ryan Mark Lambert

BIRTHDATE: March 29, 1971

BIRTHPLACE: Cleveland, Ohio

HEIGHT: 5'5"

WEIGHT: 120 lbs.

HAIR: Dark brown

EYES: Brown

FAMILY: Dad, Robert; mom, Marlene; younger brother, Jay

CURRENT RESIDENCE: Simi Valley, California

FAVORITE FOOD: Pasta salad

FAVORITE DRINK: Cherry Coke

FAVORITE ACTOR: James Dean

FAVORITE ACTRESS: Meryl Streep

FAVORITE SHOWS: *General Hospital*, *The Cosby Show*

FAVORITE ROCKERS: Madonna, Tears for Fears, Mr. Mister

FAVORITE PLACE TO VISIT: Disneyland

FAVORITE SPORT: Wrestling

FAVORITE CITY: Chicago, Illinois

FAVORITE PASTIME: Playing pool

INSTRUMENT PLAYED: Guitar

TELEVISION: *Kids, Inc.*, guest appearances on *Sidekicks* and *Silver Spoons*

MOVIE: *The Monster Squad*

IDEAL GIRL: "I'm attracted to a girl who likes to have fun," he says. "I'm not saying she has to be wild, but she should be outgoing."

WHERE TO WRITE TO RYAN: Ryan Lambert
      c/o Vincent Sorrentino
        Management
      P.O. Box 691651
      Los Angeles, CA 90069

ROB LOWE

There was never a time when Rob Lowe didn't consider a career in acting. "Most kids go through a phase where they want to be an astronaut or something," he says. "It was never like that with me. I always kind of knew that I wanted to be an actor."

Born in Charlottesville, Virginia on March 17, 1964 to Barbara and Charles Lowe, Rob was seven years old when his parents divorced. After his mother's second divorce, when Rob was thirteen, she moved Rob, his brother Chad and half-brothers Micah and Justin to California. There she met and married her third and present husband, Dr. Steve Wilson.

Rob was bit by the acting bug at age eight when he went to see the play *Oliver*. Immediately, he asked his parents to sign him up. He found acting to be a way to escape and he starred in dozens of plays and appeared in local TV shows. When he was fourteen, he signed with a talent agent and began doing commercials.

His breakthrough role was playing Eileen Brennan's oldest son in the short-lived TV series *A New Kind of Family*. After receiving his high school equivalency diploma, Rob enrolled in UCLA's Motion Picture Department. But landing the role of Sodapop Curtis in *The Outsiders* put a temporary hold on his college plans.

After *The Outsiders*, Rob decided to stick with acting and his next film, *Class*, was his first comedy. "It was scary doing comedy for the first time," he says, "because I had to be 110 percent every day." His film credits include *Hotel New Hampshire*, *St. Elmo's Fire*, *About Last Night* and *Square Dance* and prove that Rob can tackle any kind of role. With parts in *Illegally Yours* and *Masquerade* as well as the part of 50s legend Eddie Cochran, this handsome actor admits, "I'm going for the highest level of success in this business."

ROB LOWE'S VITAL STATISTICS

FULL REAL NAME: Robert Hepler Lowe

NICKNAME: Rob, Shecky Showbiz

BIRTHDATE: March 17, 1964

BIRTHPLACE: Charlottesville, Virginia

HEIGHT: 5'10"

WEIGHT: 130 lbs.

HAIR: Brown

EYES: Blue

FAMILY: Parents, Charles and Barbara, are divorced; brother, Chad; stepbrothers, Micah and Justin

FIRST TV SERIES: *A New Kind of Family*

TV MOVIES: *Thursday's Child, A Matter of Time, Schoolboy Father*

FILMS: *The Outsiders, Class, Hotel New Hampshire, Oxford Blues, St. Elmo's Fire, Youngblood, About Last Night, Square Dance, Illegally Yours, Masquerade*

FAVORITE SPORTS: Baseball, basketball, tennis

FAVORITE ACTOR: Clint Eastwood

FAVORITE STORE: Charivari

FAVORITE SINGER: Bruce Springsteen

PET: One dog, Wolfie

CAR: Gray 928S Porsche

BEST FRIENDS: Emilio Estevez, Tom Cruise

FAVORITE PASTIMES: Photography, going to the beach, watching cartoons

IDEAL GIRL: "The ideal person would know about music, film, basically a fair amount about the arts."

WHERE TO WRITE TO ROB: Rob Lowe
c/o ICM
8899 Beverly Blvd.
Los Angeles, CA 90048

ANDREW McCARTHY

Andrew McCarthy is very serious about his acting career now, but it wasn't always that way. While studying drama at New York University, Andrew decided to go on an audition because he needed to "kill the afternoon." As he remembers, "A friend of mine read that there was a general casting call and told me about it. I was bored that day, so I tried out for the part. Just me and a couple of hundred other young actors," he adds with a laugh.

On the day he was to register for classes, Andrew was called back and won his first role, as Jonathan Ogner in *Class*. The praise he received from critics for his performance of the awkward new student at an upper class prep school ultimately paved the way for Andrew's very successful career in movies.

A fan of Tennessee Williams' plays, Andrew was born in Westfield, New Jersey on November 29, 1962. Following his performance in *Class*, blue-eyed Andrew starred in the films *Dear Lola* and *Heaven Help Us*. With roles in *Pretty in Pink*, *Mannequin* and his most recent *Less Than Zero*, Andrew says his all-time favorite role was Kevin Dolenz in *St. Elmo's Fire* because "I can relate to him."

Between projects, Andrew likes relaxing in his two-room apartment in Greenwich Village with his pet cat Zelma. He enjoys playing tennis and golf and taking a pretty girl to a movie or play.

Looking ahead, Andrew says he plans on acting for a very long time. "I don't know what I'd do if I didn't act," he offers. "It lets my feelings show. And that's why I love it!"

ANDREW McCARTHY'S VITAL STATISTICS

FULL REAL NAME: Andrew T. McCarthy

BIRTHDATE: November 29, 1962

BIRTHPLACE: Westfield, New Jersey

HEIGHT: 5'8"

WEIGHT: 140 lbs.

HAIR: Brown

EYES: Blue

FAMILY: Dad, Stephen, a stock analyst; mother, Dorothy; brothers, Steve (27), Pete (25) and Justin (15)

FILMS: *Class*, *Heaven Help Us*, *St. Elmo's Fire*, *Pretty in Pink*, *Mannequin*, *Kansas*, *Less Than Zero*

FAVORITE ACTORS: James Dean, Montgomery Clift, Robert Duvall

FAVORITE BOOKS: Anything written by Tennessee Williams and Ernest Hemingway

FAVORITE SINGER: Bruce Springsteen

FAVORITE FOOD: Chinese, pizza, cheeseburgers

FAVORITE CLOTHES: Jeans, jackets, polo shirts, sneakers

BEST FRIENDS: Emilio Estevez, Rob Lowe, Judd Nelson

WORST FAULTS: He worries too much and is a little superstitious

FAVORITE THING TO DO ON A DATE: Go to a movie or play

CURRENT RESIDENCE: His own apartment in the Greenwich Village area of New York

DESCRIPTION OF ANDREW'S APARTMENT: Two rooms filled with his favorite things which include a giant Bruce Springsteen poster on the wall and a faded Oriental rug on the floor.

LITTLE KNOWN FACT: Andrew has two scars. One is above his right eyebrow and he got it when he fell out of the car as a two-year-old. The other is on his left cheek and he received it during a hockey game.

WHERE TO WRITE TO ANDREW: Andrew McCarthy
c/o William Morris Agency
151 El Camino Drive
Beverly Hills, CA 90212

RALPH MACCHIO

With a string of successful screen roles under his belt, Ralph Macchio has emerged as one of the leading young actors working in American film today. Born on November 4, 1961 in Dix Hills, New York, Ralph possesses an undeniable boy-next-door charm and brings a special brand of dedication to each of his roles.

At an early age, Ralph found himself drawn to music and dance. "I was a big fan of Gene Kelly," he says. He began taking dancing lessons and performed in local New York productions all through high school. It was during a show at Hofstra University that young Ralph was spotted by his manager, Marie Pastor, who immediately signed him.

His quick success in his first film, *Up The Academy*, led to Ralph's being signed as a series regular on TV's *Eight is Enough*. Roles in *The Outsiders* and TV movies followed, but it was not until he played Daniel in *The Karate Kid* that Ralph gained enormous popularity.

He had a small role in *Teachers* and played Eugene Martone in *Crossroads* for a change of pace, but was anxious about playing Daniel again for *The Karate Kid Part II*. "What I did," says Ralph, "was to try to take a little bit of the East Coast humor I had grown up with and give it to Daniel. I guess it must have worked."

Ralph took a break from movies and decided to accept a role in the play *Cuba and His Teddy Bear* opposite his idol, Robert DeNiro. After finishing this limited run on Broadway, he snuck away for a little time off. He married his childhood sweetheart Phyllis Fiero on April 5, 1987 in a small, private ceremony. He also signed to star in *The Karate Kid Part III*, as well as a film called *Distant Thunder* with John Lithgow.

Talented Ralph plans on acting for a long time. "I'm very much involved in acting," he confides. "And I plan to be involved for as long as I can see. It's an endless medium. You never reach a point where you can't go anywhere!"

RALPH MACCHIO'S VITAL STATISTICS

FULL REAL NAME: Ralph George Macchio, Jr.

BIRTHDATE: November 4, 1961

BIRTHPLACE: Dix Hills, New York

HEIGHT: 5'9"

WEIGHT: 135 lbs.

HAIR: Brown

EYES: Deep, dark brown

FAMILY: Dad, Ralph, Sr.; mom, Rosalie; brother, Steven

MARITAL STATUS: He married his childhood sweetheart Phyllis Fiero on April 5, 1987.

FILMS: *Up The Academy*, *The Outsiders*, *The Karate Kid*, *Teachers*, *Crossroads*, *The Karate Kid Part II*, *Distant Thunder*

TV SERIES: Ralph played Jeremy on *Eight is Enough*

TV MOVIES: *Journey to Survival*, *Dangerous Company*, *The Three Wishes of Billy Grier*

FAVORITE ACTOR: Robert DeNiro

FAVORITE SINGERS: Bruce Springsteen, Billy Joel

FAVORITE SPORTS: Hockey, tennis

FAVORITE FOOD: Italian — especially pizza and lasagna!

FAVORITE DRINKS: Milk and fruit juices

FAVORITE COLOR: Blue

FAVORITE VACATION SPOT: Hawaii

BIGGEST DISAPPOINTMENT: That a movie he really cared about, *Crossroads*, was not a hit and only garnered mediocre reviews

MOST PRIZED POSSESSIONS: The guitar he played in *Crossroads* and his stereo.

SECRET FEAR: That he will be typecast as *The Karate Kid*.

SECRET DESIRE: To become a writer!

WHERE TO WRITE TO RALPH: Ralph Macchio
c/o Columbia Pictures
711 Fifth Ave.
New York, NY 10022

LOU DIAMOND PHILLIPS

The role of Ritchie Valens in *La Bamba* was easy for Lou Diamond Phillips. The 25-year-old actor knew a lot about the music of Valens and other 50s rockers before he tried out for the film. "When I was growing up, I listened to oldies, while all my friends were listening to disco," says Lou.

He was born in the Philippines on February 17, 1962, an only child. His father Gerald Upchurch died when he was just two years old. He was raised by his mother, Lucy, and step-father, George Phillips, in Dallas, Texas. Acting throughout high school and college, he graduated from the University of Texas in 1984 and spent two years acting on the stage and teaching.

He appeared in a bit part on the TV show *Dallas* and made three films, *Angel Alley*, *Harley* and *Trespasses*, before winning the prized role of Ritchie Valens in *La Bamba*. At first, he auditioned for Ritchie's bad brother Bob, but the producer and casting people knew immediately that he was perfect for the lead.

To prepare for the role, Lou took guitar lessons and gained fifteen pounds. The director strapped a Walkman to his head and told him to listen to Valens' music. "I'd wake up in the middle of the night singing *La Bamba*," says Lou, laughing.

On June 27, 1987, before the film was released, Lou married his girlfriend of two years, Julie Cyphers. Julie is an assistant director and the couple say they have no plans to start a family. "Around our home, it's Academy Awards before babies," grins Lou.

Looking ahead, he wants to continue acting and has already finished two upcoming films, *Walking on Water* and *Dakota*. "I get intense gratification out of making movies," he says. "I love watching things come to life."

LOU DIAMOND PHILLIPS' VITAL STATISTICS

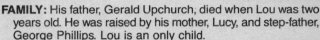

FULL REAL NAME: Lou Diamond Phillips

BIRTHDATE: February 17, 1962

BIRTHPLACE: The Philippines

HEIGHT: 6′

WEIGHT: 160 lbs.

HAIR: Brown

EYES: Brown

FAMILY: His father, Gerald Upchurch, died when Lou was two years old. He was raised by his mother, Lucy, and step-father, George Phillips. Lou is an only child.

MARITAL STATUS: On June 27, 1987, he married Julie Cyphers, who is an assistant director.

INSTRUMENT PLAYED: He learned guitar for *La Bamba*

EDUCATION: He has a degree in theater from the University of Texas

FAVORITE ACTOR: Dustin Hoffman

FAVORITE PASTIMES: Writing, drawing, watching movies

FAVORITE SPORT: Skiing

FAVORITE FOOD: Mexican

FAVORITE MUSIC: "I was always a 50s buff," he says. "I listened to oldies when everyone else was listening to disco."

MOVIES: *Angel Alley, Harley, Trespasses, La Bamba, Walking On Water, Dakota*

TELEVISION: Guest appearance on *Dallas*

LITTLE KNOWN FACT: Originally, Lou auditioned for the role of Ritchie's bad brother Bob before winning the lead in *La Bamba*

FUTURE GOALS: To produce, act, direct and have a stable home life and a permanent address

WHERE TO WRITE TO LOU: Lou Diamond Phillips
c/o Columbia Pictures
Columbia Plaza South
Burbank, CA 91505

RIVER PHOENIX

Movie audiences fell in love with River Phoenix in *Stand By Me*. It turned the talented actor into a star, but River had been acting professionally since the age of nine. Born in a log cabin in Madras, Oregon, he spent his early childhood traveling all over South and Central America with his parents, who were archbishops in the Children of God religious cult in Venezuela.

When his parents left the cult, River and his sister, Rainbow, sang on the streets of Los Angeles for money. The family, which includes three other children, lived out of the back of a VW which was converted into a camper by River's dad. Remembering those days, the blue/gray-eyed actor says, "A lot of people made fun of us because we were very poor." At age nine, he wanted to help his family and decided acting was the way to do it.

He began his career in commercials, but wanted to break into television and movies. "Commercials were too phony for me," he reflects. "I just didn't like it, even though it helped us pay the rent."

He went on numerous auditions and won roles in various television movies and shows. At fourteen, he got his first break on the big screen, playing the young scientist Wolfgang Muller in *The Explorers*. Next came *Stand By Me*, which River says "is the first film I totally liked working in" and he followed that with *The Mosquito Coast* opposite Harrison Ford.

He has filmed three new movies, *A Night in the Life of Jimmy Reardon*, *Little Nikita* and *Running on Empty* back-to-back and the demand for him keeps growing. He dates his *Mosquito Coast* co-star Martha Plimpton and wants to continue playing exciting and challenging roles. An accomplished musician, he plays guitar and keyboards and looks forward to "recording an album of my own music someday!"

RIVER PHOENIX'S VITAL STATISTICS

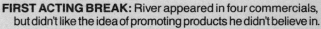

FULL REAL NAME: River Jude Phoenix

BIRTHDATE: August 23, 1970

BIRTHPLACE: Madras, Oregon

HEIGHT: 5'8½"

WEIGHT: 135 lbs.

HAIR: Dark blond

EYES: Blue/gray

FAMILY: Dad, John; mom, Arlyn; three sisters, Rainbow, Liberty, Summer; one brother, Leaf

FIRST ACTING BREAK: River appeared in four commercials, but didn't like the idea of promoting products he didn't believe in.

TV SHOWS: Guest appearances on *Family Ties*, *Hotel*, *It's Your Move*

TV MOVIES: *Celebrity*, *Robert Kennedy and His Times*, *Seven Brides for Seven Brothers*, *Surviving*, *Circle of Violence*

AFTERSCHOOL SPECIAL: *Backward — The Riddle of Dyslexia*

FILMS: *Explorers*, *Stand By Me*, *The Mosquito Coast*, *A Night in the Life of Jimmy Reardon*, *Little Nikita*, *Running on Empty*

FAVORITE COLOR: Blue

FAVORITE FOOD: Anything vegetarian, especially mangos, oranges, coconuts

FAVORITE DRINK: Orange juice

FAVORITE ACTOR: Robert DeNiro

FAVORITE PASTIMES: Playing his guitar, going on family outings

IDEAL GIRL: Someone nice. "That's what attracts me," he says.

BIGGEST THRILL: He wrote the theme song to *Jimmy Reardon*

PET PEEVE: Being treated differently because he's an actor. "It annoys me," he says. "I'm just an everyday person doing a job."

WHERE TO WRITE TO RIVER: River Phoenix
c/o Clein and Feldman
554 North Huntley Drive
West Hollywood, CA 90048

MOLLY RINGWALD

Molly Ringwald plunged into show business at a very early age. Born on February 18, 1968, red-haired Molly is the youngest daughter of blind jazz musician Bob Ringwald.

At age four, she began singing professionally and at five, she performed in front of 2,000 people at the California State Fair and Exposition. Later she recorded two songs, *Oh, Daddy!* and *I Wanna Be Loved By You*, with her dad's Great Pacific Jazz Band.

In the same year, she auditioned for and won a role in the Truman Capote play *The Glass Harp*. Molly made her singing debut on television when she guest-starred on *The New Mickey Mouse Club* and soon won the part of Kate in the West Coast production of *Annie*. She was a regular on the first season of *Facts of Life* and gained such recognition in her first film, *Tempest*, she received a Golden Globe nomination.

In 1983, she met writer/producer/director John Hughes and worked with him on three films. With her sensitive portrayals of teenagers in *Sixteen Candles*, *The Breakfast Club* and *Pretty in Pink* she secured a name for herself in Hollywood.

The actress, who has dyed her hair black, blonde, red and pink, says she's not a typical teen. "I never wanted to be," asserts Molly, who dates Beastie Boy Adam King "Ad-Rock" Horovitz.

Her latest film is *The Pickup Artist* and her next project is the movie version of the Broadway play *To Gillian On Her Birthday*. Of her future, Molly says with a smile, "I'd like to play someone zany, wacky and ridiculous. Playing a part totally different from me would be a lot of fun."

MOLLY RINGWALD'S VITAL STATISTICS

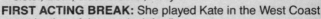

FULL REAL NAME: Molly Ringwald

BIRTHDATE: February 18, 1968

BIRTHPLACE: Sacramento, California

HEIGHT: 5'4"

WEIGHT: 105 lbs.

HAIR: Dark Red

EYES: Brown

FAMILY: Dad, Bob; mom, Arlene; older sister, Beth; older brother, Kelly

FIRST ACTING BREAK: She played Kate in the West Coast production of the musical *Annie*

TELEVISION: *The New Mickey Mouse Club*, *Facts of Life* (she was a regular during its first year), TV movie *Surviving*, Showtime Special *Johnny Appleseed*

MOVIES: *Spacehunter: Adventures in the Forbidden Zone*, *Sixteen Candles*, *The Breakfast Club*, *Pretty in Pink*, *The Pickup Artist*, *For Keeps*

FAVORITE MUSICIANS: The Bangles, Prince, Bruce Springsteen

FAVORITE SPORT: Swimming

FAVORITE FOOD: Onion rings in ketchup, crab cakes, raspberries

FAVORITE COLOR: Pink

FAVORITE CLOTHES: Jeans and tank tops

MOLLY HAS DATED: Actors Anthony Michael Hall, Ricky Paull Goldin and Dweezil Zappa

MOLLY IS NOW DATING: The Beastie Boys' King Ad-Rock

ROLE THAT IS CLOSEST TO HER REAL LIFE SELF: *Pretty in Pink's* Andie Walsh

ROLE THAT WAS FURTHEST FROM HER REAL LIFE SELF: *The Breakfast Club's* Claire Standish. "She's the girl you grew up hating," notes Molly.

FUTURE GOALS: To continue acting and to write, sing and direct someday.

WHERE TO WRITE TO MOLLY: Molly Ringwald
120 El Camino Dr., Suite 104
Beverly Hills, CA 90212

ALLY SHEEDY

Ally Sheedy's talents are endless. Only twenty-five years old, she has starred in eight major motion pictures, written a best-selling children's book and contributed articles to such publications as *The Village Voice*, *The New York Times* and *Ms.* magazine.

Born in New York, Ally is the daughter of a marketing executive father and a writer/literary agent mother. She attended the Ecole Francaise and The Bank Street School and performed for eight years with the American Ballet Theatre. Before she was eighteen, Ally had already done commercials, off-off Broadway and After-school Specials.

On her eighteenth birthday, she moved to Los Angeles and enrolled in the University of Southern California. In 1983, she made her film debut in *Bad Boys* opposite Sean Penn. That same year, she played Jennifer, the strong-minded, self-possessed friend of computer whiz Matthew Broderick in *WarGames*. In her next film, *Oxford Blues*, she played the only woman on the English college's male rowing team. Ally touched filmgoers and critics with her portrayal of Allison Reynolds in *The Breakfast Club*. She followed that up with performances in *St. Elmo's Fire*, *Twice in a Lifetime*, *Blue City*, *Short Circuit* and her most recent comedy, *Maid to Order*.

Though Ally, who dates musician Steve Ross, recently returned to her love of writing, working on her first adult novel, she says she wants to continue making movies.

"It's wonderful to be able to embrace so many people's experiences," she enthuses. "For me, that's what movies are all about."

ALLY SHEEDY'S VITAL STATISTICS

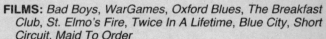

FULL REAL NAME: Ally Sheedy

BIRTHDATE: June 13, 1962

BIRTHPLACE: New York City

HEIGHT: 5′7″

WEIGHT: 125 lbs.

HAIR: Light brown

EYES: Hazel

CURRENT RESIDENCE: Los Angeles, California

FILMS: *Bad Boys*, *WarGames*, *Oxford Blues*, *The Breakfast Club*, *St. Elmo's Fire*, *Twice In A Lifetime*, *Blue City*, *Short Circuit*, *Maid To Order*

WORST JOB: "Working in an ice cream parlor one summer. I had to wash dishes and sweep the floor all day long."

FAVORITE ACTRESS: Katharine Hepburn

FAVORITE AUTHORS: F. Scott Fitzgerald, D.H. Lawrence, Anne Tyler

FAVORITE TV SHOWS: Animal shows on public television

WORST TIME OF HER LIFE: "High school and when I saw myself in *WarGames*. I felt confused and inadequate. Now I feel I've walked through the unknown and come out on the other side!"

BEST TIME OF HER LIFE: "This past year has been great!"

OTHER ACHIEVEMENTS: At age six, Ally performed with the American Ballet Theatre. At twelve, she wrote a best-selling children's book called *She Was Nice to Mice*. She also has contributed articles to *The New York Times* and *The Village Voice*.

FUTURE GOALS: She wants to keep acting. Right now, she is writing her first adult novel.

WHERE TO WRITE TO ALLY: Ally Sheedy
c/o New Century Vista Film Company
2020 Avenue of the Stars
Los Angeles, CA 90067

CHARLIE SHEEN

Charlie Sheen, the handsome star of movies like *Lucas* and *Platoon*, admits he's always had show business in his blood. The son of actor Martin Sheen and film producer, Janet, Charlie is no stranger to movie sets. "I've learned more by sitting and talking with my dad than spending a year with the best acting teacher in the world," he says proudly. "In fact, my whole family is entirely supportive of one another. Maybe if we were up for the same parts it would be different, but we're all different types."

As a young boy, Charlie filmed super-8 shorts which starred himself, his brothers and friends Chris Penn and Chad Lowe. Charlie was really bitten by the acting bug after making his debut in *The Execution of Private Slovik* with his dad, after which he spent eight months with him working as an extra in *Apocalypse Now*. An avid baseball fan, Charlie says, "I guess that's when I decided I should give acting a shot. Having spent all that time with dad filming *Apocalypse Now*, I realized there was more to life than baseball."

After deciding to go into acting seriously, he won roles in numerous films including *Grizzly II — The Predator*, *Red Dawn*, *The Boys Next Door* and *Lucas*. But he didn't become a star until *Platoon* came along. Of his role in the Oscar-winning Vietnam drama, Charlie says, "It was the role of a lifetime. We were doing things we didn't think we were capable of doing — as actors or individuals. They took us to the edge, but didn't push us over it."

Charlie's latest film, *Wall Street*, has proven how talented this hazel-eyed actor is. Eventually, says Charlie, he would like to become a director, but right now acting is most important to him. "It's important to me to establish myself as an actor. I know the rest will come in time."

CHARLIE SHEEN'S VITAL STATISTICS

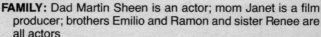

FULL REAL NAME: Carlos Irwin Este-vez (he chose the name Charlie Sheen because "I'm hardly ever called Carlos which would have gone better with Estevez. Charlie Estevez didn't sound right either so I took my dad's stage name and it sounded great!")

BIRTHDATE: September 3, 1965

BIRTHPLACE: New York City

HAIR: Dark Brown

EYES: Hazel

HEIGHT: 5'11"

WEIGHT: 145 lbs.

FAMILY: Dad Martin Sheen is an actor; mom Janet is a film producer; brothers Emilio and Ramon and sister Renee are all actors

FIRST ACTING BREAK: At nine, Charlie was an extra in his father's TV movie *The Execution of Private Slovik*

TV MOVIE: *Silence of the Heart*

MOVIES: *Apocalypse Now, Grizzly II — The Predator, Red Dawn, The Boys Next Door, Lucas, Platoon, Three For The Road, Wall Street*

FAVORITE SPORT: Baseball

FAVORITE FOOD: "Anything!"

FAVORITE PASTIME: Filming 8mm movies starring friends Chris Penn and Chad Lowe

THE IDEAL GIRL FOR CHARLIE: "I look for the three C's," he says. "Coolness, calmness and composure."

HOW CHARLIE DESCRIBES HIMSELF: "The captain of my own ship, the consummate bachelor."

FUTURE GOALS: Charlie wants to direct someday soon. He is writing a screenplay called *How To Eat and Drive* and he says, "It's stupid, really, but look at *Porky's* and *Revenge of the Nerds*. If those films can get made and make millions, I can put something on paper and film it."

WHERE TO WRITE TO CHARLIE: Charlie Sheen
4866 Fountain Avenue
Los Angeles, CA 90029

ERIC STOLTZ

"Acting is what I do best," says Eric Stoltz sincerely. "I love performing. It's what moves me." Eric fell in love with acting at the age of ten when he stumbled into a summer theatre on vacation.

He was born in American Samoa in the South Pacific and began studying the trumpet and piano at an early age. His parents moved Eric and his two older sisters to Santa Barbara, California when Eric was eight and he began appearing in local theatre productions.

At eighteen, he enrolled in the University of Southern California in the Theatre Arts Department and studied acting for two years. He soon started winning parts in films and TV movies and had key roles in *Next of Kin*, *A Killer in the Family*, *Fast Times at Ridgemont High*, *Thursday's Child* and *The Wild Life*. His most significant movie appearance was as Rocky Dennis in the critically acclaimed *Mask*.

Of all his roles, he considers Keith Nelson in John Hughes' *Some Kind of Wonderful* his favorite. "I was very excited about being chosen to play Keith," says Eric. "He's a great character and it was a very special movie."

Eric has found himself very busy this year filming his upcoming movies, *Emerald*, *Sister, Sister*, *Lionheart* and *Haunted Summer*. Though blue-eyed Eric loves acting, he dreams of becoming a director someday. To get some idea of what it's like working behind the camera, he took a job as a production assistant on Rob Lowe's movie *Illegally Yours*. Though he admits his job was "mostly to bring Rob Lowe his coffee," it did teach him quite a bit about moviemaking and may ultimately have helped to prepare this ambitious guy for another successful career.

ERIC STOLTZ'S VITAL STATISTICS

FULL REAL NAME: Eric Stoltz

BIRTHDATE: September 22, 1962

BIRTHPLACE: American Samoa in the South Pacific

HEIGHT: 5'10"

WEIGHT: 160 lbs.

HAIR: Red

EYES: Blue

FAMILY: His parents are teachers who raised Eric and his two older sisters in the South Pacific. They moved to Santa Barbara, CA when Eric was eight years old.

MOVIES: *Fast Times at Ridgemont High, The Wild Life, Mask, Some Kind of Wonderful, Lionheart, Sister, Sister, Haunted Summer, Emerald*

TELEVISION: *Next of Kin, A Killer in the Family*

CURRENT RESIDENCE: He has two apartments. One in Paris, France, the other in Los Angeles

FAVORITE PASTIME: Going to art museums

INSTRUMENTS PLAYED: Piano, trumpet

IDEAL GIRL: Someone serious and independent

PAST GIRLFRIENDS: He dated Ally Sheedy and was linked with Cher during the time they filmed *Mask*

LITTLE KNOWN FACT: He doesn't believe in Valentine's Day

QUOTE ON FAME: "Fame is a very strange beast."

FUTURE GOALS: To become a film director. He already gained some experience working as a production assistant on Rob Lowe's film *Illegally Yours*.

BEST EXPERIENCE AS AN ACTOR: "I was very excited about being chosen to play Keith in *Some Kind of Wonderful*. Working with John Hughes was like a dream come true."

WHERE TO WRITE TO ERIC: Eric Stoltz
c/o Paramount Pictures
5555 Melrose Avenue
Los Angeles, CA 90038

WIL WHEATON

Wil Wheaton received rave reviews for his role as Gordie Lachance in the sleeper hit *Stand By Me*. It was the first major role for the hazel-eyed actor, who had been acting since the age of seven.

The oldest child of Rick and Debbie Wheaton was born on July 29, 1972 and his first professional job was in a television commercial for Jello-O Pudding Pops opposite Bill Cosby. That led to TV movies like *A Long Way Home* and *The Defiant Ones*. He had a small role in the movie *The Last Starfighter*, but it was *Stand By Me* that turned Wil into a star.

"I knew it was a good film," he says. "But I really never expected it to receive so much critical acclaim." Playing the role of the budding writer inspired Wil to begin writing his own short stories.

"I write them for my friends," he explains. "I picked it up when I played Gordie and I've never stopped." After *Stand By Me*, Wil was cast as the legendary magician Harry Houdini in the Disney Sunday movie *Young Harry Houdini*. He also nabbed the starring role in the thriller *The Farm* and is one of the regulars on the TV series *Star Trek: The Next Generation*.

When he isn't working or going to school, Wil enjoys the beach, music by the Beastie Boys and Stephen King novels. He says the best part of being an actor is "meeting new people and being able to play someone else." As for the worst part, brown-haired Wil simply says, "That's easy. I hate getting up early in the morning!"

WIL WHEATON'S VITAL STATISTICS

FULL REAL NAME: Richard William Wheaton III

BIRTHDATE: July 29, 1972

BIRTHPLACE: Burbank, California

HEIGHT: 5'9"

WEIGHT: 125 lbs.

HAIR: Brown

EYES: Hazel

FAMILY: Dad, Rick; mom, Debbie; younger brother, Jeremy; younger sister, Amy

CURRENT RESIDENCE: Sun Valley, California

PETS: Three cats, Ziggy, Grady and Ocean

FAVORITE SPORTS: Surfing, skiing, jogging

FAVORITE PASTIME: Writing *Twilight Zone*-ish short stories

FAVORITE COLOR: Green

FAVORITE PLACE: The beach. "I love listening to the waves, watching the ocean," he says.

FIRST ACTING BREAK: At age seven, he appeared opposite Bill Cosby in a Jell-O Pudding Pops commercial

TV MOVIES: *A Long Way Home*, *The Defiant Ones*, *Young Harry Houdini*

FILMS: *The Last Starfighter*, *Stand By Me*, *The Farm*

TELEVISION: *Star Trek: The Next Generation*, Guest appearances on *St. Elsewhere*, *Highway to Heaven*, *Family Ties*

THE FIRST THING HE NOTICES ABOUT A GIRL: Her eyes

PET PEEVE: His own singing and dancing

LITTLE KNOWN FACT: Wil is a magician and card tricks are his specialty. "I *always* have a deck of cards with me wherever I go," he says.

WHERE TO WRITE TO WIL: Wil Wheaton
c/o Wilpower
Box 12567
La Crescenta, CA 91214

PART THREE
ROCK STARS

MAGS FURUHOLEM

The youngest member of A-ha is Magne Furuholem, who was born on November 1, 1962. At six years of age, Mags' father was killed in a plane crash. He was raised by his grandfather and mother in his native Oslo, Norway.

"My father was an extremely important influence on me," says Mags. "Because he died when I was very young, the most vivid image I have is of him playing away on his trumpet."

Though Mags credits his father with giving him the inspiration to go into music, his grandfather also gave young Mags encouragement. A professional musician himself, Mags' grandfather gave the young would-be musician an electric guitar and amplifier which Mags says "really got me involved with rock music."

With determination, Mags learned to play the guitar, but switched to the piano and eventually mastered it. He and his childhood friend, Pal Waaktaar, would make music every afternoon in Mags' basement. "Fortunately my mother supported us and didn't mind listening to us banging out music," he says with appreciation.

When Mags, Pal and Morten moved to London to try and get their band going, they all lived under one roof. "We had a gas leak in the bedroom," recalls Mags, "and had only two beds for three people."

This blond-haired rock star says his life as a member of A-ha is fun. With a third album on the way, he honestly admits, "The farther we get, the farther we want to go!"

MAGS FURUHOLEM'S VITAL STATISTICS

FULL REAL NAME: Magne Furuholem

NICKNAME: Mags, Magsaroonie

BIRTHDATE: November 1, 1962

BIRTHPLACE: Oslo, Norway

HEIGHT: 6'1"

WEIGHT: 160 lbs.

HAIR: Blond

EYES: Blue

FAMILY: Mags was raised by his mother and grandfather. His father died when Mags was six years old. Mags has one younger sister, Line, and two half-brothers, Thorstein and Trygve.

INSTRUMENT PLAYED: Keyboards

FAVORITE SPORT: Football

FAVORITE COLORS: Blue and "technicolor colors in old films."

FAVORITE FOOD: Junk food

FAVORITE MUSICIANS: The Beatles, The Doors

FAVORITE TYPE OF CLOTHING: T-shirts, Levi's jeans and jackets

FAVORITE SPORTS: Windsurfing, race car driving

FIRST BAND: Britches (with Pal Waaktaar)

HIS METHOD FOR WRITING SONGS: "Any way I can think of!"

ODD JOBS BEFORE JOINING A-HA: Substitute teacher, art exhibit assistant

BIGGEST THRILL: Going up in a hot air balloon

BIGGEST DISAPPOINTMENT: "Disappointments are always big!"

CAR: A big, old Rover

WHERE TO WRITE TO MAGS: Mags Furuholem/A-ha
c/o Warner Bros. Records
75 Rockefeller Plaza
New York, NY 10022

MORTEN HARKET

When Morten Harket was growing up in Norway, he never thought he'd make music his future career. Though he learned to play piano and guitar, his real love for music did not develop until high school.

Morten is the son of a doctor and a teacher, and his hobbies as a child centered around his love of nature. He began growing orchids and collecting butterflies at age ten and admits that the beautiful town he lived in was his inspiration for loving the outdoors.

"I grew up in Kongsberg, Norway, which is a very old mountain town," says Morten. "I always thought it was thrilling to study butterflies or watch reindeer play."

By the time Morten was eighteen, he started listening to rock 'n' roll and says, "it completely knocked me out! Right away, I wanted to be in a band!" Morten gained his experience by forming a band he named Ansaps, which he says "is a type of orchid."

In 1982, he met Pal Waaktaar and Mags Furuholem at a school dance and they talked of forming a three man band. Leaving Norway for London, Morten says, "We knew no one, had no contacts. We just had some ideas, a few songs and figured we'd take it from there."

Though it wasn't an overnight success story for Morten and his two bandmates, Mags and Pal, they were soon signed to a Warner Bros. Records contract. With the success of their first LP, *Hunting High and Low*, they were on their way to the top.

Of his future, Morten says, "There are going to be exciting things happening with us in the future. I'm especially looking forward to making a movie."

MORTEN HARKET'S VITAL STATISTICS

FULL REAL NAME: Morten Harket

BIRTHDATE: September 14, 1959

BIRTHPLACE: Kongsberg, Norway

HEIGHT: 6′

WEIGHT: 160 lbs.

HAIR: Brown

EYES: Blue

FAMILY: Three brothers, Grunvald (29), Hako (25), Kjetil (20); one sister, Ingunn (23); his dad is a doctor and his mom is a teacher.

FIRST AMBITION: To become a doctor

FAVORITE MUSIC: Rhythm and blues

FAVORITE MUSICIAN: Otis Rush

FAVORITE FOOD: "My mom's cooking!"

FAVORITE HOBBY: Growing orchids

FAVORITE CLOTHES: Leather jackets, pants and wristbands

FIRST BAND: Ansaps

MOST PRIZED POSSESSION: "My camera!"

HOW MORTEN WOULD DESCRIBE HIMSELF: "I get embarrassed easily and I'm very critical of myself!"

MARITAL STATUS: Single

WHAT KIND OF GIRL DOES MORTEN LIKE?: "I'm attracted to a girl who is a genuinely nice person," he says.

BEST ADVICE HE'S EVER RECEIVED: "My mom told me once, 'Stay naive and absent-minded!'"

INSTRUMENTS PLAYED: "I'm the lead singer of the band (A-ha), but I do play piano and guitar."

WHERE TO WRITE TO MORTEN: Morten Harket/A-ha
c/o Warner Bros. Records
75 Rockefeller Plaza
New York, NY 10019

PAL WAAKTAAR

A-ha's songwriter Pal Waaktaar's interest in music emerged when he was just eleven years old. "I used to make myself a drum set out of cardboard every week," says Pal. "Actually, I got to be quite good at it."

Born on September 6, 1961 in Oslo, Norway, Pal switched to the guitar at age fourteen because it helped him write songs. "The first songs I wrote were mainly about love," confides Pal, who had been introduced to music by his parents. They took him to the opera when he was very young and the first single he ever bought was a song from the opera *Carmen*. After that, he was inspired by shows like *Hair* and rock bands like Deep Purple and The Doors.

He met fellow A-ha band member Mags at age ten and they formed a band called Britches which lasted until they graduated from high school. Growing up together, Pal and Mags were determined to become professional musicians and used to practice every day after school in Mags' basement.

Pal says his "greatest source of support came from my older sister, Tongje. She really backed me all the way."

Though this handsome green-eyed rocker found himself doing odd jobs like putting pills into boxes and selling tickets in a subway in England, Pal soon came up with the ultimate name for his band. He scribbled the word A-ha in his notebook and when Morten, who had joined Pal and Mags, saw it, the three decided it was the perfect name.

Pal is happy about the success of A-ha because he says his favorite thing in the whole world is "writing songs and working on new ones."

PAL WAAKTAAR'S VITAL STATISTICS

FULL REAL NAME: Pal (pronounced Paul) Waaktaar

BIRTHDATE: September 6, 1961

BIRTHPLACE: Oslo, Norway

HEIGHT: 6'1"

WEIGHT: 145 lbs.

HAIR: Blond

EYES: Green

FAMILY: His dad is a pharmacist; his mom works in communications; one sister, Tongje

FIRST BAND: Britches (with Mags)

FAVORITE FOOD: Bagels with goat cheese

FAVORITE AUTHORS: Franz Kafka, Knut Hamsun

FAVORITE COLOR: Blue

FAVORITE SPORTS: Soccer, ping pong

FAVORITE MUSICIANS: The Doors, U2, Judy Garland (singing *Over the Rainbow*)

LEAST FAVORITE JOB: Cleaning house

PETS: "Just Mags and Morten!"

WHAT DOES PAL HATE?: Hayfever!

WHAT DOES PAL LOVE?: "My family!"

INSTRUMENTS PLAYED: Drums, keyboards, bass, guitar

THE BIGGEST INFLUENCE ON HIS LIFE: "My greatest source of support came from my older sister, Tongje. She's backed me all the way."

FAVORITE CLOTHES: Levi's jeans, leather jackets and leather wristbands

WHERE TO WRITE TO PAL: Pal Waaktaar/A-ha
c/o Warner Bros. Records
75 Rockefeller Plaza
New York, NY 10022

JON BON JOVI

Jon Bon Jovi, the handsome lead singer of the hot band Bon Jovi, is riding a wave of success. Though the climb was a little bumpy for the 5'10" superstar, he enjoyed every step he took up the ladder.

John Frank Bongiovi, Jr. was born on March 2, 1962 in Sayreville, New Jersey. "Bongiovi is an Italian name," he says. "To be more precise, it's Sicilian. My ancestors were immigrants to America in the good old-fashioned way. They tried to make some bucks like everybody else."

Jon's dad made his bucks as a hairdresser; his mom, Carol, runs a flower shop and he has two brothers, Matt and Tony.

Jon learned how to play the guitar at age fourteen when he asked a neighborhood guitarist for lessons. He played in the short-lived band Atlantic City Expressway, where he first met Bon Jovi band member David Bryan. At seventeen, Jon's cousin, Tony gave him a job sweeping floors at Power Station Studios in New York City. A chance meeting with Bruce Springsteen changed the young musician's entire life.

Bruce was producing an album for Gary U.S. Bonds and asked Jon to give him one of his songs. Bonds recorded Jon's tune *Don't Leave Me Tonight* and the ambitious singer/songwriter was on his way!

Upon writing a song called *Runaway*, Jon recorded it and sent it to a local DJ, who began playing it on the radio. The song caught on with listeners and PolyGram Records took notice of Jon. They signed him up without a band, but Jon didn't waste any time gathering together four of the best musicians in New Jersey. With two albums behind them that have sold a million copies, *Bon Jovi* and *7800° Fahrenheit*, there is no stopping Jon and his fiery bandmates. The mega-success of their third album, *Slippery When Wet*, finds Bon Jovi on top of the world. Of the band's future, Jon simply states, "We're here to stay!"

JON BON JOVI'S VITAL STATISTICS

FULL REAL NAME: John Frank Bongiovi, Jr.

NICKNAME: Captain Kidd

BIRTHDATE: March 2, 1962

BIRTHPLACE: Sayreville, New Jersey

HEIGHT: 5'10"

WEIGHT: 150 lbs.

HAIR: Brown

EYES: Blue

FAMILY: Dad John is a retired hairdresser though he still does Jon's hair; mom Carol runs a flower shop; Jon has two younger brothers, Tony (20) and Matt (12)

MUSICAL INFLUENCES: Bruce Springsteen, Van Halen, The Babys

FIRST RECORD HE EVER BOUGHT: *Blood On The Tracks* by Bob Dylan

EARLY JOBS: Transcribing tapes for editors, working in a shoe store, fast food restaurant and junkyard

FAVORITE FOOD: Italian, Mexican and junk food

FAVORITE COLORS: Purple, red

FAVORITE HOBBIES: Baseball, driving and lifting weights

FAVORITE ACTOR: Clint Eastwood

FAVORITE BANDS: U2, Tom Petty, Little Steven

ALBUMS: *Bon Jovi, 7800° Fahrenheit, Slippery When Wet*

FANTASY CAR: Porsche

WHAT KIND OF GIRL DOES JON LIKE?: "Someone with an independent streak."

PET: A small dog named Scruffy

FUTURE GOALS: "I plan on being around as long as the Rolling Stones. Every day we get better as a band and we learn more about what it takes to be around for 20 years."

WHERE TO WRITE TO JON: Jon Bon Jovi
                         c/o PolyGram Records
                         810 Seventh Avenue
                         New York, NY 10019

DAVID BRYAN

David Bryan first met Jon Bon Jovi when they were sixteen years old. "I met him through my cousin," he remembers. "This band called Atlantic City Expressway needed a keyboardist and I was the only one with a Hammond organ. Jon said, 'Bring him in!' Atlantic City Expressway was a real R & B style band."

David Brian Rashbaum was born on February 7, 1962 in Edison, New Jersey. "Music was always a big part of my life," says the blue-eyed rocker. "At seven, I studied piano and continued to take lessons for thirteen years."

Although David enjoyed the experience of playing in the Atlantic City Expressway band, he left music temporarily to study medicine at Rutgers University. When that didn't work out, he went back to his original love and studied at Juilliard for one year.

In 1983, Jon began recruiting musicians for a new band and he called his old friend David. After recording the band's first album, Dave legally changed his name to David Bryan because he felt his original name "was too ethnic." What he didn't realize was that another David Bryan was on the FBI's hit list for armed robbery and David found himself constantly being questioned. "Every time I check in on a flight, all hell breaks loose," he says ruefully.

As Bon Jovi's keyboardist, David is living out his dream of making rock 'n' roll his career. Of his future with the most successful band in rock today, light-brown-haired David notes, "This is just the beginning for us. We have to continue to work harder and do something different each time."

DAVID BRYAN'S VITAL STATISTICS

FULL REAL NAME: David Brian Rashbaum (he changed it legally to David Bryan)

BIRTHDATE: February 7, 1962

BIRTHPLACE: Edison, New Jersey

HEIGHT: 6'

WEIGHT: 155 lbs.

HAIR: Light brown

EYES: Blue

FAMILY: Dad, Ed, is a jazz trumpeter; sister, Michele

EDUCATION: John P. Stevens High School in Edison, New Jersey; he studied pre-med for two years at Rutgers University and attended Juilliard for one year

MUSICAL INFLUENCES: Chopin, Bach, Beethoven, Rick Wakeman

FIRST BAND: Transistor

INSTRUMENTS PLAYED: Keyboards, guitar, bass, drums and trumpet

FIRST CONCERT ATTENDED: Kiss

FAVORITE FOOD: Lobster

FAVORITE COLOR: Blue

QUOTE: "We paid our dues, we lived in the depths of deprivation and got turned down by just about every record company."

HOW HE FEELS ABOUT SUCCESS: "I couldn't be happier. I'm knocking on every piece of wood I see."

THE FUTURE OF BON JOVI: "The ball is really rolling great and we're going with the flow. We're going to stay out there til the big hook comes down to grab us."

WHERE TO WRITE TO DAVID: David Bryan — Bon Jovi
c/o PolyGram Records
810 Seventh Avenue
New York, NY 10019

RICHIE SAMBORA

As Bon Jovi's ace guitarist and songwriter, Richie Sambora is dedicated to his career. He fell in love with music at the age of seven when he began taking accordion lessons. At fourteen, he decided to switch to the guitar because it helped him write his own music. "I taught myself, but I did take some courses in music theory," brown-haired Richie offers.

After he graduated from high school, the Woodbridge, New Jersey native began playing clubs and joined numerous bands. During his years on the club circuit, he met Bon Jovi band member Alec John Such. They worked together in a group called Message, but the band lasted only a few months. The two friends went their separate ways for two years, but Alec didn't forget Richie's fantastic guitar playing.

In 1983, while Richie was doing session work in Chicago, he received a phone call from Alec. "He told me, 'Tico and I are helping this band called Bon Jovi and The Wild Ones.' He told me to come and check them out. I went to see them and thought, 'There's something here!'"

Though the group already had a guitarist, Richie and Jon Bon Jovi hit it off immediately and he soon took over as the band's guitarist. He also began writing most of Bon Jovi's songs with Jon. In fact, Richie says, the first day they got together they wrote two of the songs that appear on the first Bon Jovi album.

Richie says he's the "try-anything type with the guitar. I'll hit it, turn it upside down and hit the walls with it." Though he'd love to give acting a try someday, he knows his heart will always be in music. He loves being part of rock's hottest band and simply states with a grin, "I love my job!"

RICHIE SAMBORA'S VITAL STATISTICS

FULL REAL NAME: Richard Sambora

BIRTHDATE: July 11, 1961

BIRTHPLACE: Woodbridge, New Jersey

HEIGHT: 6'1"

WEIGHT: 155 lbs.

HAIR: Brown

EYES: Brown

FAMILY: Richie is an only child. His parents were dancers.

MUSICAL INFLUENCES: Eric Clapton, Johnny Winter, Jeff Beck

FIRST BAND: Rebel

INSTRUMENTS PLAYED: Guitar, keyboards, drums and bass

FAVORITE COLOR: Red

FAVORITE TV SHOW: *Late Night with David Letterman*

FAVORITE MUSIC: Everything but opera and disco

FAVORITE ACTRESS: Jamie Lee Curtis

FAVORITE FOOD: Hamburgers, pizza

DEFINITION OF FAME: "Fame hasn't changed me, *I've* changed fame."

RICHIE'S FIRST GUITAR: It was a Gibson SG and it was broken during one of Richie's early gigs. Someone tripped over a cord and split the neck. "I glued it together because I couldn't afford to get it fixed," says Richie. "But it was never the same."

THE ONE THING HE'D LIKE TO TRY: "Acting," he says. "Just to see if I could do it. Not that I want to do it now."

HOW WOULD RICHIE DESCRIBE HIMSELF?: "I'm very friendly and I like to party. But I'm also very private."

HAS SUCCESS CHANGED RICHIE?: "Well, now we have a place and stay in nice hotels. But we're still the same guys we were before."

WHERE TO WRITE TO RICHIE: Richie Sambora — Bon Jovi
c/o PolyGram Records
810 Seventh Avenue
New York, NY 10019

ALEC JOHN SUCH

Even after years of playing in various bands, Alec John Such still wasn't prepared for the success Bon Jovi has had with their third album, *Slippery When Wet*. "I only imagined this in my dreams," says Bon Jovi's brown-eyed bass player. "This is phenomenal!"

Alec, who was born on November 14, 1952, grew up in a musical family. His mother played the violin and his father played a Hungarian gypsy instrument called a cumbalon. It seemed only natural that Alec would pursue a career in music.

Alec began studying the violin at age eight and says his mother kept after him if he didn't practice every day after school. "Tears used to run down my face and onto the violin," laughs Alec today.

When he was a teenager he took up the bass and began playing in bands all through his high school years. After high school, he went to college for two years, but left to make money as a musician.

Alec gained a reputation as one of the best bass players in the business. When he joined Bon Jovi in 1983, he was already a seasoned pro.

He says the chemistry among the Bon Jovi band members is part of the reason for the group's success. "Before a show we stretch, slap five to get into it," grins Alec. "It's like being on a team."

Alec loves making music so much that he has learned to take the good with the bad. His only pet peeve is "recording. I just don't like it," he volunteers. "I work much better playing live!"

ALEC JOHN SUCH'S VITAL STATISTICS

FULL REAL NAME: Alex John Such

BIRTHDATE: November 14, 1952

BIRTHPLACE: Perth Amboy, New Jersey

HEIGHT: 5'7"

WEIGHT: 130 lbs.

HAIR: Brown

EYES: Brown

FAMILY: Alec's parents are professional musicians; he has an older brother, Kenneth, and one sister, Dianne

MUSICAL INFLUENCES: Beatles, Tim Bogart, Jack Bruce

FIRST BAND: The Cellar Dwellers

INSTRUMENTS PLAYED: Guild basses, violin

FIRST RECORD BOUGHT: *Love Me Do* by the Beatles

FAVORITE FOOD: Everything except creamed corn

FAVORITE ACTOR: Humphrey Bogart

FAVORITE COLOR: Black

FAVORITE BANDS: Motley Crue, Vanilla Fudge

HOBBIES: Racing cars and motorcycles, skiing, sailing, flying

FAVORITE VACATION SPOT: Cayman Islands

FUTURE GOALS: To make tons of money

QUOTE: "My life is charmed, I think. It's like magically protected from harm. I've had good luck."

WHERE TO WRITE TO ALEC: Alec John Such – Bon Jovi
c/o PolyGram Records
810 Seventh Avenue
New York, NY 10019

TICO TORRES

Tico Torres was the fourth musician to join Bon Jovi. He says he is "ecstatically happy with the way things are going." After being part of so many bands before, Tico felt Bon Jovi had something special right from the beginning.

He was born Hector Torres on October 7, 1954 in New York City. Though he was an only child, Tico's parents took in Cuban refugees while he was growing up, so he always had someone around to talk to.

His interest in music began at an early age. "I had a snare drum when I was nine and began playing with bands at sixteen. I played with over one hundred bands," says Tico, whose musical influences were The Beatles, Frank Zappa, Phil Collins and Cream.

When his friend, Alec John Such, told him about the band Jon was trying to get together, Tico was interested. He had seen Jon singing in a club in New Jersey and "thought he was a great performer. After I toured with Bon Jovi, I knew the band had zest," he remarks.

Tico wants to continue working as Bon Jovi's drummer, but admits he'd also like to try his hand as a solo artist someday. He's composing more now and sometimes collaborates with musicians outside Bon Jovi such as Jeff Carlisi of .38 Special. Tico is most interested in writing jazz and says someday he'd like to try producing and record a solo album.

But right now, he's having a great time working as a musician for the hottest band in rock today. "I don't mind being in the studio or going on tour," he explains. "I like them both 'cause I love playing drums!"

TICO TORRES' VITAL STATISTICS

FULL REAL NAME: Hector Torres

NICKNAME: The Hitman

BIRTHDATE: October 7, 1954

BIRTHPLACE: New York City

HEIGHT: 5'8"

WEIGHT: 150 lbs.

HAIR: Brown

EYES: Brown

FAMILY: His widowed mother is a secretary. Tico is an only child.

MUSICAL INFLUENCES: Beatles, Frank Zappa, Phil Collins, Cream

FIRST BAND: Cold Sweat

INSTRUMENTS PLAYED: Drums. Tico uses Pearl drums, Paiste cymbals, custom 5b sticks

FAVORITE SPORT: Fishing

FAVORITE MOVIE: *E.T.*

FAVORITE COLOR: Black

FAVORITE FOOD: Pork sandwich

ONE-WORD DESCRIPTION OF HIMSELF: "Determined."

HOW HE FEELS ABOUT FAME: "Fame hasn't changed me, but it has made me wiser about a lot of things."

MOST EMBARRASSING EXPERIENCE: Falling off his drums onstage.

BEST CONCERT HE'S EVER ATTENDED: Phil Collins

FUTURE GOALS: "We have to come up with a new record that won't let people down. I never want any of our fans to be disappointed. We have to keep working and striving without burning out."

WHERE TO WRITE TO TICO: Tico Torres – Bon Jovi
c/o PolyGram Records
810 Seventh Avenue
New York, NY 10019

SIMON LeBON

Before Duran Duran, Simon LeBon had already been an actor since the age of five. His mother, Anne, who wanted to become a singer herself, worked hard for her oldest son's career. "I think my mother hoped I would fulfill her ambitions," recalls blue-eyed Simon.

His early career included roles in commercials and stage plays and he began taking acting classes after his regular school day was over. This ambitious go-getter wasn't the kind of kid who was satisfied with going to school and playing with toys. He acted all through elementary school and during high school, became interested in music.

By the time he graduated, he knew he wanted to pursue a career in music and began singing in punk rock bands while attending Birmingham University. The thing that changed his life was an audition for a new dance-rock band called Duran Duran. "We must have auditioned hundreds of vocalists before Simon came in and shone like a diamond," says John Taylor.

Simon was so excited when he was chosen as the group's lead vocalist that he celebrated by writing a song called *The Sound of Thunder*. It appeared on their debut album, *Duran Duran*. Though they soon became the hottest band in rock, Simon admits it took a while before they caught on. "We did three very unsuccessful tours in the United States," he remembers. "And we came away thinking we'd never make it in America."

After splitting from Duran Duran to be part of Arcadia, Simon, who is married to Yasmin Parvenah, is now back to singing lead vocals for the newly reformed Duran Duran. Commenting on their new sound, he says, "It's much simpler. We're just concentrating on good songs now."

SIMON LeBON'S VITAL STATISTICS

FULL REAL NAME: Simon John Charles LeBon

BIRTHDATE: October 27, 1958

BIRTHPLACE: Bushey, Hertfordshire, England

HEIGHT: 6'1"

WEIGHT: 160 lbs.

HAIR: Sun-streaked blond

EYES: Blue

FAMILY: Dad, John; mom, Anne; younger brothers, David and Jonathan

MARITAL STATUS: Married to Yasmin Parvenah

PET: Dog named Sam

FIRST JOB: At age five, Simon appeared in a TV commercial for a laundry soap called Persil

FIRST BAND: Dog Days

FAVORITE FOODS: Indian, seafood

FAVORITE DRINKS: Wine, lemonade

FAVORITE TIME OF DAY: Sunset

FAVORITE SPORTS: Swimming, sailing

FAVORITE MUSICIANS: The Doors, David Bowie

FAVORITE FLOWER: Rhododendron

FAVORITE PLACE: On stage singing

FAVORITE CITIES: New York and Sydney, Australia

FAVORITE PASTIME: Sailing

SECRET DESIRE: "I hope through my music, I'm able to add some fun to people's lives," he says. "Give them a chance to recognize difficult parts of their own lives and let them know they're not alone."

WHERE TO WRITE TO SIMON: Simon LeBon
Duran Duran
273 Broad Street
Birmingham B12DS England

NICK RHODES

As a child, Nicholas James Bates used to earn extra money from his parents by washing the family car and mowing the lawn. At ten, Nick informed his parents, Roger and Sylvia, that he dreamed of becoming a rock star when he grew up.

Born on June 8, 1962 in Birmingham, England, he and boyhood friend John Taylor spent their early years playing music. When they graduated high school, they formed a dance-rock band called Duran Duran.

In June 1981, their debut album, *Duran Duran*, was the hottest album of the year and it was followed by *Rio* in 1982. Their third LP, *Seven and the Ragged Tiger*, was released in November, 1983 and the following year, *Arena* joined their string of album hits.

The popular band also released three videos between 1983 and 1984 and everyone thought Duran Duran would last forever. But in 1985, the group split down the middle and half the guys formed Arcadia, while the others formed The Power Station. Now back with John and Simon in Duran Duran, Nick admits that the split "was probably the best thing that ever happened to us. We're all stronger now because of it!"

Nick is happily married to Julie Anne Friedman and they are proud parents of a baby boy. Looking to his future, green-eyed Nick would someday like to direct films. An ace photographer, he has had exhibitions of his work all over the world and he even published a book of his polaroid photos. Of Duran Duran's successful *Notorious* album and world tour, Nick says, "We've grown up and so have our fans. It seems like the people who have stuck by us have grown with us." And that's the key to success in music!

NICK RHODES' VITAL STATISTICS

FULL REAL NAME: Nicholas James Bates

NICKNAME: Ringo

BIRTHDATE: June 8, 1962

BIRTHPLACE: Birmingham, England

ASTROLOGICAL SIGN: Gemini

HEIGHT: 5'9"

WEIGHT: 130 lbs.

HAIR: Blond

EYES: Green

EARLY JOB: Nick used to earn extra money from his parents (Roger and Sylvia) by washing the family car and mowing the lawn.

FAVORITE FOOD: French

FAVORITE DRINKS: Champagne, Perrier

FAVORITE HAIR PRODUCTS: Vidal Sassoon shampoo and conditioner

FAVORITE SCHOOL SUBJECTS: Music and art

FAVORITE POSSESSIONS: His gold ring which his mother gave him and his 35 mm camera.

FAVORITE CHILDHOOD MEMORY: "When I was 13, I became very interested in art and used to go to this great gallery called the Icon in Birmingham, England. My memories of that place are still vivid."

MARITAL STATUS: He and his wife, Julie Anne Friedman, have a son

LITTLE KNOWN FACT: He claims he dreams in living color.

INSTRUMENT PLAYED: Keyboards

SECRET DESIRE: He'd like to direct films one day.

SELF-DESCRIPTION: "I'm a very relaxed person. I never need to panic."

WHERE TO WRITE TO NICK: Nick Rhodes
Duran Duran
273 Broad Street
Birmingham B12DS England

JOHN TAYLOR

Jean and Jack Taylor always knew their son, John, would pursue some form of music. In fact, John says they knew even before he did.

Nigel John Taylor was born on June 20, 1960 and spent his early childhood reading car magazines, painting metal toy soldiers and playing all the popular music of the day on his stereo. At fourteen, he got his first guitar and his interest in *listening* to music turned into determination to play, too!

John became more involved with music and it was at this time he met Nicholas James Bates or Nick Rhodes, as he was later known. John and Nick found they had a lot in common and quickly became the best of friends. "We were the only kids on our block who were hip enough to own a copy of David Bowie's *Rise and Fall of Ziggy Stardust* LP," John remembers. Their friendship eventually led to the formation of a band they called Duran Duran, with a title taken from the film *Barbarella*.

Three more members joined the group, and Duran Duran became the hottest band in rock from 1981 to 1984, with a new best-selling album released every year. But hot on the heels of their worldwide exposure, the guys decided to split up and subsequently formed two separate bands, Arcadia and The Power Station.

In 1987, John, Nick and Simon LeBon felt it was time to return to the band that had made them famous, and they reformed Duran Duran. John says the split helped the band members, and admits that now "Duran Duran will be together for a long time. I promise if we do break up eventually, I won't be the one to do it," he adds with a grin. And that's music to the ears of his countless fans.

JOHN TAYLOR'S VITAL STATISTICS

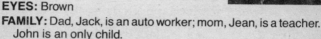

FULL REAL NAME: Nigel John Taylor

NICKNAMES: JT, Tigger (from *Winnie-the-Pooh*)

BIRTHDATE: June 20, 1960

BIRTHPLACE: Birmingham, England

HEIGHT: 6'1"

WEIGHT: 145 lbs.

HAIR: Brown

EYES: Brown

FAMILY: Dad, Jack, is an auto worker; mom, Jean, is a teacher. John is an only child.

GIRLFRIEND: Renee Simonson

INSTRUMENT PLAYED: Bass guitar

PETS: Dog, Rolf and cat, Chaz

FAVORITE ROCKERS: David Bowie, The Bangles, Billy Idol

FAVORITE MOVIES: All James Bond movies

FAVORITE TV SHOWS: *Dynasty*, *Dallas*

FAVORITE CLOTHES: Baggy pants and jackets

FAVORITE CARTOON CHARACTERS: "Probably Tigger from *Winnie-the-Pooh*, but I also like Donald Duck, and Dino from *The Flintstones*."

FAVORITE NIGHT OUT: Dining and dancing

MOST PRIZED POSSESSIONS: His James Bond videos and James Bond car, an Aston Martin

EARLIEST CHILDHOOD MEMORY: "I remember my fourth birthday and getting an orange dump truck. Before the age of four, things are a little hazy."

THE THING HE LOVES TO DO WHEN HE'S HOME: Talking on his portable telephone.

WHERE TO WRITE TO JOHN: John Taylor
Duran Duran
273 Broad Street
Birmingham B12DS England

COREY HART

"I knew I wanted to write songs and sing back when I was fourteen years old," says rocker Corey Hart, who has had success with his three albums, *First Offense*, *Boy in the Box* and *Fields of Fire*. His dedication to the music business has never let up and through his years of working his way to the top, he has never surrendered.

With those two words in the back of his mind at all times, Corey became a star. Ironically, it was his song *Never Surrender* which catapulted him to the top of the charts. "I wanted to get my message across to people through that song," says Corey. "Because it's always worked for me."

At seventeen, blue-eyed Corey recorded his first demo tape and during a Billy Joel concert, sent it backstage to Billy's saxophonist Richie Cannata. Richie was immediately impressed with Corey's music and what followed was a year in which Richie helped Corey to build his career. Working with Richie as his mentor, Corey recorded a debut album and was on his way up the charts in no time.

"I'm very involved with my career. I know music will always be a big part of my life," says Corey, who admits that he still gets excited when he hears one of his tunes on the radio.

Corey wears a leather bracelet that's fastened with a padlock, which his girlfriend Erika gave to him and to which she holds the key. "If you ever see me without it, you know there's trouble ahead," says Corey with a mischievous look in his eye.

Though Corey is hot on vinyl, he's even hotter on stage. His concerts are simply dynamite and this ambitious superstar says, "There's nothing that can compare to the feeling I have after I get off the stage. The concerts are the ultimate for me and nothing can match them!" After going to see one of his electrifying shows, his many fans feel exactly the same way!

COREY HART'S VITAL STATISTICS

FULL REAL NAME: Corey Mitchell Hart
BIRTHDATE: May 31, 1962
BIRTHPLACE: Montreal, Canada
HEIGHT: 5'10"
WEIGHT: 145 lbs.
HAIR: Brown
EYES: Blue
FAMILY: Parents Robert and Mindy divorced when Corey was thirteen years old; sister, Donna; brothers, Robbie, Michael and Stephen
CURRENT RESIDENCE: Montreal, Canada
CAR: He still drives his first car, an old Mazda
FAVORITE MUSICIANS: Elvis Presley, Police, Eurythmics
FAVORITE FOOD: Chinese
FAVORITE DRINK: Tea with honey
FAVORITE CLOTHES: T-shirts, jeans, leather jackets
ALBUMS: *First Offense, Boy in the Box, Fields of Fire*
PET PEEVE: "I don't like being photographed!"
FEELINGS ON FANS: "I take great pride in what my fans have to say. It's very important for me to pick up a batch of mail and read through it."
SELF-DESCRIPTION: "I'm a very intense and sensitive person!"
FUTURE GOALS: "I want to continue to grow in all I do as an artist, a songwriter and a performer."
WHERE TO WRITE TO COREY: Corey Hart
c/o Shades
3405 Thimens Blvd.
St. Laurent, Quebec
Canada H4R IV5

WHITNEY HOUSTON

As a young girl, Whitney Houston used to sing gospel songs at her church in Newark, New Jersey. The only daughter of gospel singer Cissy Houston, Whitney grew up in a musical family. "Everyone in my family sings," she says. "It's just part of our lives."

Although she is close to her father, John, and older brothers, Gary and Michael, Whitney says her greatest inspiration was her mother. "Whenever I think of my success, I thank God for my mother," she confides. "She gave me the confidence, drive and state of mind to go the distance."

Her first album, *Whitney Houston*, was a huge success for the brown-eyed singer. It not only spawned four hit singles, *You Give Good Love*, *Saving All My Love For You*, *How Will I Know* and *The Greatest Love of All*, but it also won Whitney two American Music Awards and a Grammy for Best Female Pop Vocalist.

Despite her sudden stardom, Whitney stayed level-headed about the business and immediately dove into working on her follow-up LP. "I'm not the kind of person who says to the world, 'I'm a star,'" she reflects. "Money doesn't make you better than anyone else. Having Cissy Houston for my mother and Dionne Warwick for my cousin, I've been around this all my life and I'm accustomed to what it's all about."

Her second album, simply titled *Whitney,* already has two top ten hits, *I Wanna Dance With Somebody* and *Didn't We Almost Have It All*. It was the first album by a woman to enter the charts at number one and Whitney's sold-out concert tour has proven she'll stay number one. She loves performing on stage and says the feeling she gets is "a feeling beyond comparison. It's so exciting!"

WHITNEY HOUSTON'S VITAL STATISTICS

FULL REAL NAME: Whitney Elizabeth Houston

NICKNAMES: Nippy, Whit, Lizzy

BIRTHDATE: August 9, 1964

BIRTHPLACE: Newark, New Jersey

HEIGHT: 5'8"

WEIGHT: 120 lbs.

HAIR: Brown

EYES: Brown

FAMILY: Dad, John, works for the Mayor of Newark, New Jersey; mom, Cissy, is a gospel singer; two older brothers, Gary and Michael

FIRST AMBITION: First she wanted to be a teacher, then a veterinarian

FIRST SINGING BREAK: At age fifteen, Whitney sang with her mother, Cissy Houston, a gospel singer in the New Hope Baptist Church Choir in New Jersey.

FIRST CAREER: Modeling, but Whitney left because "when I was a model, I wasn't looked at for what I was, but for what I had on."

PETS: Two cats, Misty and Marilyn

FAVORITE MOVIES: *Back to the Future*, *Gandhi*

FAVORITE TV SHOW: *The Cosby Show*

FAVORITE COLOR: Lavender

FAVORITE PLACES: The beach, Japan, Caribbean

FAVORITE SINGERS: Stevie Wonder, Aretha Franklin

FAVORITE CLOTHES: At home — sneakers, t-shirts and jeans. When she goes out she likes wearing mini skirts, fringed boots and eye-dazzling jewelry.

ALBUMS: *Whitney Houston*, *Whitney*

GREATEST INFLUENCE: Her mother

WHERE TO WRITE TO WHITNEY: Whitney Houston
c/o Arista Records
8370 Wilshire Blvd.
3rd Floor
Beverly Hills, CA 90211

BILLY IDOL

Billy Idol the man is quite different from Billy Idol the rock star. Born William Broad on November 30, 1955 in Stanmore, North London, England, he attended Sussex University and majored in English literature. A serious student, Billy couldn't ignore his love of music and decided to pursue it as a career. "It's my whole life," he says honestly. "I've always believed that music gives you a grasp on what people are all about and why they do things."

Before breaking into the music business, the young singer gained his experience by playing in the bands Generation X and Chelsea. His smooth singing style and "punk" good looks were the perfect combination for a future rock star and before long, Billy signed a record contract.

His first two albums, *Billy Idol* and *Rebel Yell,* were huge successes, and many expected a third LP to follow quickly. But Billy decided to wait a year and a half before releasing *Whiplash Smile*.

"When I'm making a record, I take a long time because I'm thinking of my fans," he says. "They are spending hard-earned cash on my records and you've got to give them something that will sound good in ten years." His *Whiplash Smile* album proved his devotion to quality music even though his songs weren't as hard-hitting as on his previous albums.

When Billy isn't writing, recording or touring, he is content to live his life in his favorite city — New York. Since his breakup with longtime girlfriend Perri Lester, he hasn't dated anyone steadily, but he looks forward to getting married and having children. "I'm working hard now so I can spend time with them once I have them," he smiles. "They'd have good fun with me, I think."

BILLY IDOL'S VITAL STATISTICS

FULL REAL NAME: William Broad

BIRTHDATE: November 30, 1955

BIRTHPLACE: Stanmore, North London, England

HEIGHT: 5′11″

WEIGHT: 160 lbs.

HAIR: Blond

EYES: Hazel

CURRENT RESIDENCE: New York City

FAVORITE SINGER: Prince

FAVORITE FOOD: Anything vegetarian

FAVORITE DRINK: Chocolate milk

FAVORITE HOBBY: Reading

FAVORITE SPORT: Bowling

FAVORITE TV SHOW: *Star Trek*

SECRET DESIRE: "I'd like to have kids one day!"

ALBUMS: *Billy Idol*, *Rebel Yell*, *Whiplash Smile*, *Vital Idol*

LITTLE KNOWN FACT: Billy uses the name William Alucard when he registers in hotels. Alucard is Dracula spelled backwards.

SECRET SUCCESS FORMULA: "My aim has always been to make sincere rock music, great records and to enjoy myself."

FEELINGS ON FANS: "I realize the personal position being a recording artist puts me in with people — as a sort of a friend. I've met lots of fans who think of me and my music that way. That's an exciting feeling!"

WHERE TO WRITE TO BILLY: Billy Idol
c/o Chrysalis Records
645 Madison Avenue
15th Floor
New York, NY 10022

MICHAEL JACKSON

The Jackson Five were the hottest group of the early 1970's. They began their careers playing clubs and in 1967, Gladys Knight and the Pips told Motown Records about them. Two years later, Diana Ross and the Supremes introduced them on ABC-TV's *The Hollywood Palace* and the young stars were born.

Michael Joseph Jackson, the group's lead singer, was always determined. Belting out the hits, *ABC*, *Got To Be There* and *I Want You Back*, Michael and his brothers released over ten albums in their first three years. In 1972, Michael got a taste of recording solo when he sang the theme song *Ben* from the film of the same name. A solo career was still years into his future, though, as he continued recording with his brothers throughout the 1970's.

Michael and younger brother Randy combined their talents by writing the hit single, *Shake Your Body Down To The Ground* and Michael continued to compose. Setting out on his own in 1978, he starred in his first movie, *The Wiz*, opposite Diana Ross. In 1979, he teamed with Quincy Jones for his first solo album, *Off The Wall*, and three years later released the biggest selling album in history, *Thriller*. He was presented with twenty-four awards for this album and many wondered if Michael could ever top it.

Before bouncing back onto the music scene with his current hit album, *Bad*, Michael embarked on his most ambitious project to date. He lent his acting, singing and dancing talents to the 3-D short musical film *Captain E-O*, which runs continuously in Disneyland and Walt Disney World.

Although multi-talented Michael wants to make music in the future, he would also like to do another motion picture. His goals are endless and he is determined to attain every one!

MICHAEL JACKSON'S VITAL STATISTICS

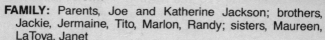

FULL REAL NAME: Michael Joseph Jackson

BIRTHDATE: August 29, 1958

BIRTHPLACE: Gary, Indiana

HEIGHT: 5'11"

WEIGHT: 135 lbs.

HAIR: Black

EYES: Dark brown

FAMILY: Parents, Joe and Katherine Jackson; brothers, Jackie, Jermaine, Tito, Marlon, Randy; sisters, Maureen, LaToya, Janet

PETS: Seven-foot boa constrictor named Muscles and several exotic pets such as a lama named Louis, peacocks, pheasants and deer. His favorite is a chimp named Bubbles

CURRENT RESIDENCE: Encino, California

ALBUMS: *Off The Wall, Thriller, E.T. The Extra-Terrestrial* (Michael sang one song and narrated the story of E.T.), *Bad*

FAVORITE BOOK: *Peter Pan*

FAVORITE MOVIE: *Captains Courageous*

FAVORITE ACTRESS: Katharine Hepburn

FAVORITE ACTOR: Charlie Chaplin

FAVORITE FOOD: Michael is a strict vegetarian

FAVORITE MUSIC: Classical, folk, old Spanish music and 60's Motown

FAVORITE PLACE TO VISIT: Disneyland

CAR: Rolls-Royce blue Silver Shadow

FUTURE GOALS: "I still want to make records but I also want to do films," he says. "That's how I want to spend the next few years."

WHERE TO WRITE TO MICHAEL: Michael Jackson
c/o Epic Records
51 West 52nd Street
New York, NY 10019

JOAN JETT

Rock and roll star Joan Jett leaped onto the big screen as Patti Rasnick in *Light of Day*. Playing Michael J. Fox's sister, Joan won the most sought-after part in Hollywood but has no plans to become an actress.

"I'm a musician," she says. "I'm going to continue making records and going on tour. I will only do another movie if the right one comes along."

Born on September 22, 1960, Joan began playing guitar at age thirteen and formed her first band, The Runaways, at fifteen. They were one of the first all-girl bands and in five years, they released six albums and toured the world. When the group disbanded in 1981, Joan formed Joan Jett and the Blackhearts and began writing songs with her manager, Kenny Laguna.

Despite her past success with The Runaways, Joan had a difficult time finding a record company to sign her new band. Finally, she and Kenny formed their own label called Blackheart and released the band's first album themselves. "We started selling the album (*Bad Reputation*) at our concerts," she says. "It sold 22,000 in four weeks and after that came *I Love Rock and Roll*."

With her catchy, hard-driving rock and roll, Joan has managed to sustain her winning streak of hit singles, releasing three albums in three years and contributing to the *Light of Day* soundtrack.

Her key to reaching the top is "you have to love music and really want it. I had a dream to perform on stage and was lucky enough to make it come true. But you have to be serious. Determination is probably the most important thing." After eleven years of performing, she is more determined than ever to continue making music. She is definitely here to stay!

JOAN JETT'S VITAL STATISTICS

FULL REAL NAME: Joan Jett
BIRTHDATE: September 22, 1960
BIRTHPLACE: Rockland, Maryland
HEIGHT: 5′4″
WEIGHT: 120 lbs.
HAIR: Black
EYES: Brown
CURRENT RESIDENCE: She lives in both Manhattan and Rockville Centre, Long Island
FIRST BAND: The Runaways
INSTRUMENT PLAYED: Guitar
ALBUMS: Six albums with The Runaways, *Bad Reputation* (released on her own Blackheart label), *I Love Rock and Roll, Album, Glorious Results of a Misspent Youth, Good Music, Light of Day* (soundtrack)
MOVIE: *Light of Day* (with Michael J. Fox)
FAVORITE CAR: Jaguar XJS
FAVORITE SINGERS: David Bowie, Billy Idol, Chuck Berry
FAVORITE BANDS: T Rex, Rolling Stones, Talking Heads, U2
FAVORITE COLOR: Red
FAVORITE CLOTHES: "I wear a lot of red and black. About six years ago, I started wearing red Pro Keds sneakers and it's become my trademark."
SELF-DESCRIPTION: Honest, friendly and soft-spoken. "A lot of people are nervous to meet me, but after a few minutes of conversation, they are much more relaxed. They realize I'm not gonna hit them," she laughs.
WHERE TO WRITE TO JOAN: Joan Jett
P.O. Box 600
Long Beach, NY 11561

CYNDI LAUPER

There is just no stopping Cyndi Lauper. Since she first burst onto the music scene with her rockin' debut hit single, *Girls Just Want To Have Fun*, she has managed to win many awards and stay on top.

Her unusual style and gypsy outfits have made people sit up and take notice. In 1984, she was awarded one of *Ms. Magazine*'s Women of the Year Awards, a Grammy, and was named Best Artist of the Year by Rolling Stone and Best Female Vocalist by Cashbox. In control at all times, she is involved in all aspects of her work including marketing her records and promoting them to radio stations.

Cynthia Ann Stephanie Lauper was born on June 20, 1953 in Astoria, Queens. Her parents divorced when she was just five years old and her mother, Catrine Dominique, raised young Cyndi and her younger brother, Butch, and older sister, Ellen. As a teenager, Cyndi began taking an interest in music. Thinking back, she admits, "I was always very comfortable when I was creating and thought I was the future."

After eight years of studying singing and sharpening her songwriting skills, Cyndi met with success in the form of her debut LP, *She's So Unusual*. She spent the next two years enjoying her newfound fame by appearing in the *We Are The World* video and recording the theme song for the film *The Goonies*. She ventured into wrestling and even managed a lady wrestler before beginning work on her follow-up LP, *True Colors*.

An abdominal operation slowed her down a bit, but she bounced back in no time with her second album and successful world tour. Cyndi's latest project is playing a beautician/psychic in the new film *Vibes*. Engaged to her manager boyfriend, David Wolff, she looks forward to having a baby someday.

CYNDI LAUPER'S VITAL STATISTICS

FULL REAL NAME: Cynthia Ann Stephanie Lauper

NICKNAME: Cyn

BIRTHDATE: June 20, 1953

BIRTHPLACE: Astoria, Queens, New York

HEIGHT: 5'3½"

WEIGHT: 108 lbs.

HAIR: Naturally a dirty blonde, but it has been many different colors

EYES: Hazel

FAMILY: Following her parents' divorce in 1958, Cyndi, her younger brother, Butch, and older sister, Ellen, were raised by their mother, Catrine Dominique

CURRENT RESIDENCE: A house in Connecticut. "It's a low-key, serene, picturesque home with a waterfall behind it," says Cyndi.

PETS: Persian cats Skeezix McPherson and Skeezix McPheasant

FAVORITE COLOR: "Plaid!"

FAVORITE HOBBIES: All crafts

FAVORITE MOVIE: All old movies

FAVORITE FOOD: Anything vegetarian

ALBUMS: *She's So Unusual, True Colors*

UPCOMING FILM: *Vibes*

MARITAL STATUS: She is engaged to manager David Wolff

FAVORITE TIME: "When I'm with David and we're together."

FUTURE GOALS: "I don't want to stop creating. I want to have kids, but I don't see how I could fit them in right now."

WHERE TO WRITE TO CYNDI: Cyndi Lauper
c/o Portrait/Epic Records
51 West 52nd Street
New York, NY 10019

JULIAN LENNON

At five years of age, John Charles Julian Lennon came home from school with a painting in his hand. It was a colorful portrait of his friend Lucy against a backdrop of a cloud of stars and he called it Lucy in the Sky with Diamonds. It became the inspiration for one of the Beatles' biggest hits.

Julian (as he was called) was born on April 8, 1963 to Beatle John Lennon and his wife, Cynthia Powell. Unfortunately before young Julian knew it, his parents divorced. His mother remarried and his father fell in love with the Japanese-American artist Yoko Ono. Beatle Paul McCartney felt sorry for John's young son and wrote the song *Hey Jude* for him.

With a growing interest in music, Julian began banging on drums and strumming on a guitar his father gave him for his eleventh birthday. Immediately thereafter, he made his recording debut playing drums on John's version of the old Lee Dorsey hit *Ya Ya* on *Walls and Bridges*.

Though he was close to his father, he didn't see too much of him while growing up. When John was killed in December, 1980, Julian coped with his feelings of grief by writing a song called *Well, I Don't Know*.

Now serious about pursuing a career in music, Julian signed with Atlantic Records in 1983 and released his debut album, *Valotte*, in 1984. The album went platinum and Julian immediately went to work on his second LP, *The Secret Value of Daydreaming*, which was released in 1986. After a world tour, he decided to take a year off before beginning work on his third album.

Though his looks and music are similiar to his famous father's, Julian has followed the long and winding road to his own success. "I'm proud to be a Lennon," he says. "That's why I feel like it's my responsibility to keep our name going in music."

JULIAN LENNON'S VITAL STATISTICS

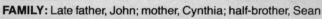

FULL REAL NAME: John Charles Julian Lennon

BIRTHDATE: April 8, 1963

BIRTHPLACE: Liverpool, England

HEIGHT: 5'9"

WEIGHT: 140 lbs.

HAIR: Brown

EYES: Brown

FAMILY: Late father, John; mother, Cynthia; half-brother, Sean

EDUCATION: Kingsmead Holylake School

MUSICAL DEBUT: Playing drums on the tune *Ya Ya* on *Walls and Bridges*

INSTRUMENTS PLAYED: Drums, keyboards and guitar

ALBUMS: *Valotte, The Secret Value of Daydreaming*

FAVORITE MUSICIANS: The Beatles, Steely Dan, Police, U2

FAVORITE SPORT: Football

FAVORITE POSSESSION: A guitar he received as an eleventh birthday present from his dad.

FAVORITE VACATION SPOT: Mexico

FAVORITE BREAKFAST: Julian starts each morning off with a hearty English breakfast of eggs, bacon, sausages and tomatoes

FAVORITE SNACK: Nestles Crunch bars

FAVORITE BEATLE BESIDES HIS DAD: Paul McCartney

MOST CHERISHED MEMORY OF HIS DAD: "Just being with him and having fun was the most important gift he gave me."

LITTLE KNOWN FACTS: He was the first child born to any of the Beatles. One of his drawings at age five inspired the Beatles song *Lucy in the Sky With Diamonds* and *Hey Jude* was written for him.

WHERE TO WRITE TO JULIAN: Julian Lennon
c/o Atlantic Records
75 Rockefeller Plaza
New York, NY 10019

MADONNA

In only a few short years, Madonna has become a very successful rock star, burning up the charts with one hit after another. But a double platinum first album, *Madonna*, and a triple platinum second album, *Like A Virgin*, weren't enough for the ambitious former dancer from Bay City, Michigan. She was determined to cross over into films and did, starring in *Desperately Seeking Susan*, *Shanghai Surprise* and *Who's That Girl?*

Born Madonna Louise Veronica Ciccone, she was named after her mother, who died when Madonna was seven years old. Her father, Anthony, remarried the housekeeper and young Madonna was placed in charge of household chores by her step-mother. Seeing herself as "the quintessential Cinderella," Madonna sought a means of escape.

She began studying ballet, modern dance and jazz and moved to New York where she won a scholarship with the Alvin Alley American Dance Theatre. She stayed with them for a few months and then joined a band called The Breakfast Club. Its leader, Steve Bray, became Madonna's boyfriend. At this time, she took her career into her own hands and recorded a demo tape of a tune called *Everybody*. A radio DJ named Mark Kamins played her song on his show and almost instantaneously, she was signed to a record deal with Sire Records.

Her three albums with Sire were major hits and her *Like A Virgin* became the longest running number one hit by a female artist in history.

Her much-publicized marriage to Sean Penn in 1985 has reportedly ended with Madonna filing for divorce. She spent the first summer away from Sean in 1987 touring the world and playing to sold-out crowds.

If all this isn't enough, Madonna also has started her own production company, Siren Films. It seems like Madonna is one performer who wants to conquer all — and does it all successfully!

MADONNA'S VITAL STATISTICS

FULL REAL NAME: Madonna Louise
Veronica Ciccone

BIRTHDATE: August 16, 1958

BIRTHPLACE: Bay City, Michigan

HEIGHT: 5'4"

WEIGHT: 120 lbs.

HAIR: Blonde

EYES: Blue

FAMILY: Mother, Madonna, died when
her daughter was seven years old; father, Anthony, remarried
his housekeeper; Madonna has seven younger brothers
and sisters, Anthony, Jennifer, Paula, Christopher, Mario,
Melanie and Martin.

EARLY JOBS: Coat check girl at the Russian Tea Room and a
model for art school classes.

MUSICAL INFLUENCES: The Archies, Gary Puckett and the
Union Gap, Bobby Sherman

FIRST MUSIC BREAK: Dance Club DJ Mark Kamins played
her song *Everybody* on his radio show

FIRST BAND: The Breakfast Club

ALBUMS: *Madonna, Like A Virgin, True Blue*

MOVIES: *A Certain Sacrifice* (a low budget film from her early
days), *Desperately Seeking Susan, Vision Quest, Shanghai
Surprise, Who's That Girl?*

FAVORITE ACTRESS: Marilyn Monroe

FAVORITE DESIGNER: Maripol

FAVORITE LIPSTICK: She *only* wears bright red lipstick

FAVORITE EYESHADOW COLOR: Gold or Pearl-colored

PET PEEVE: Undependable people

HOW SHE DESCRIBES HERSELF: "I'm tough, ambitious
and I know exactly what I want."

FUTURE GOALS: "I want to conquer the world!"

WHERE TO WRITE TO HER: Madonna
c/o Sire/Warner Bros. Records
75 Rockefeller Plaza
New York, NY 10019

RAY ACEVEDO

The day that Raymond Enrique Acevedo Kercado joined Menudo in January 1985 was the happiest day of his life. He replaced Ray Reyes and adjusted to life as a Menudo very quickly. Born on December 21, 1972, Ray was chosen for the group because of the response he generated with a single he recorded on his own. The song, a Spanish version of *She Works Hard For The Money*, was produced by Ray's dad and released independently.

Just a few weeks after joining Menudo, Ray made his recording debut on the album *Menudo* and says, "I've always liked to sing and dance." He admits his best days are the ones he spends with the other Menudo members in their Orlando, Florida home. The guys are equipped there with everything they could want. "We rehearse all our dances there," says Ray. "And record our albums. In the mornings, we do our schoolwork for three hours. It's like a resort. When I'm there, I relax and spend time in the pool."

Ray also enjoys playing basketball, reading comic books and visiting Disney World. He feels the years he has spent in Menudo have taught him independence and helped him grow up. "We go to different countries, we meet different people and we just learn how to be independent," he says.

Like his best friend, Ricky Martin, Ray also adores Menudo's many fans. "The part I like most about being in the group is definitely the girls screaming," he says with a twinkle in his eye. "I feel great when they scream because that's the way they say they love Menudo!"

Of his future, he confides, "I don't know what I want to do once I get out of the group. I want to continue to study and I'm going to go to a college in the United States. I'm just going to take one step at a time."

RAY ACEVEDO'S VITAL STATISTICS

FULL REAL NAME: Raymond Enrique Acevedo Kercado

BIRTHDATE: December 21, 1972

BIRTHPLACE: Bayamon, Puerto Rico

HEIGHT: 5'5"

WEIGHT: 130 lbs.

HAIR: Brown

EYES: Dark brown

FAMILY: Dad, Ray, Sr.; mom, Sonia; two sisters, Nilsa and Glorily

BEST FRIEND: Ex-Menudo Roy Rosello

JOINED MENUDO: January 1985, replacing Ray Reyes

FAVORITE SPORTS: Baseball, volleyball and basketball

FAVORITE HOBBY: Buying and reading comic books

FAVORITE SINGERS: Cyndi Lauper, Michael Jackson

FAVORITE PLACE TO VISIT: Disney World

FAVORITE MOVIE: *Cannonball Run*

FAVORITE DRINK: Pepsi

IDEAL GIRL: Someone who is sincere, honest and close to her family.

BIGGEST INFLUENCE ON HIS LIFE: "My parents, because they love me," he says.

SECRET DREAM: "I want to go to Australia very, very much one day."

SELF-DESCRIPTION: "I'm just a normal kid!"

WHERE TO WRITE TO RAY: Ray Acevedo
Menudo
c/o Padosa Av.
Ponce de Leon 157
Hato Rey, Puerto Rico 00913

RUBEN GOMEZ

The eighteenth and newest addition to Menudo is Ruben Gomez, who replaced Robby Rosa on May 18, 1987. When cute brown-eyed Ruben learned he was the lucky one chosen, he was very excited. "My dad told me I had been chosen," he says. "But I didn't believe him until I asked my mom and she told me it was true. I was crazed and had to go into my room to calm down," he adds, giggling.

Born on April 25, 1975 in Brooklyn, New York, Ruben had been a Menudo fan since he was nine years old. "I began sending Menudo tapes when I was nine," he offers. "But they didn't take me because I was too young. So I sent a few more and they liked my voice and called me. The next thing I knew I was the new Menudo," smiles Ruben, who lives in Manhattan with his family when he isn't working with the group.

Ruben was officially welcomed into Menudo with a press conference, which was held in Manhattan's Hard Rock Cafe. "It was the first time I saw so many cameras," he remarks. "I was interviewed in Spanish and English and everyone in the room was interested in us."

Ruben was with the group only four days before he began working on stage. His first show was at the Performing Arts Center in Puerto Rico and he admits he was a little nervous. "It was scary because I didn't know the words to the songs," he says. "But now I'm not scared anymore."

When he has some free time, Ruben loves reading comic books, playing video games and swimming. As the new kid on the block, he is looking forward to his years as a Menudo member. His favorite part so far has been "the performing and the fans. I love being around the fans!"

RUBEN GOMEZ'S VITAL STATISTICS

FULL REAL NAME: Ruben Gomez
BIRTHDATE: April 25, 1975
BIRTHPLACE: Brooklyn, New York
HEIGHT: 5'4"
WEIGHT: 108 lbs.
HAIR: Brown
EYES: Brown
FAMILY: Dad, Jose Orlando Cotti; mom, Evelyn Gomez; three step-brothers, Orlan, Ricky and Mikey

LANGUAGES SPOKEN: Spanish and English
JOINED MENUDO: May 18, 1987, replacing Robby Rosa
FAVORITE ROCKERS: Bon Jovi, Europe
FAVORITE SPORTS: Swimming, football, baseball
FAVORITE PASTIMES: Playing video games, reading comic books
FAVORITE COMIC BOOK HEROES: "My favorite comic is *X-Men*. I would like to be an X-Man. I guess I'd want to be Colossus. He's the guy who has metal all over, and no one can break through it."
HOW HE FELT ABOUT BEING CHOSEN AS A MENUDO: "Very, very excited. I was crazed," he chuckles.
LITTLE KNOWN FACTS: New York native Ruben is the first United States resident to be chosen for Menudo. All the other members were living in Puerto Rico when they were chosen for the group.
FEELINGS ON FANS: "I love being around the fans!"
HOW HE FEELS ABOUT MENUDO: "I thought it was going to be all work, work, work," he admits. "But I found that the people in Menudo are friends. We're always having fun!"
WHERE TO WRITE TO RUBEN: Ruben Gomez
Menudo
c/o Padosa Av.
Ponce de Leon 157
Hato Rey, Puerto Rico 00913

SERGIO GONZALES

On January 27, 1986, adorable Sergio Gonzales officially joined supergroup Menudo. "I was nervous when I first started," says Sergio. "But everyone really helped me out." The brown-eyed cutie had no trouble fitting in with the rest of the Menudo guys. He mastered the dance steps in a mere three weeks and quickly learned the Menudo songs in different languages.

Born on February 3, 1973, in Gainesville, Florida, Sergio moved to Puerto Rico at age seven. He began modeling and was seen in many of Puerto Rico's television commercials and ads. But his greatest moment came when he was told he was chosen to join Menudo. "I was happy when Roy Rossello, whom I replaced, decided to stay on and play the Puerto Rican countries with me," says Sergio. "I loved having him teach me and give me his support."

Although there are many reasons why Sergio likes being a Menudo, the main ones are traveling and meeting all his fans. "I love making new friends in new countries," he confides and adds that his favorite European country is Italy because "I love Italian food!"

When he has some time to himself, Sergio loves working out to the music of Madonna, playing his favorite video game TRON and practicing his synthesizer. He also enjoys dating and likes a girl who is intelligent and fun to be with. His idea of a fun date is to go to the movies and eat in a nice restaurant.

Since he joined Menudo, life has certainly changed for Sergio. But he's enjoying every minute of it because he feels his experience with the group has made him more mature and independent.

SERGIO GONZALES' VITAL STATISTICS

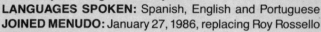

FULL REAL NAME: Sergio Gonzales, Jr.

BIRTHDATE: February 3, 1973

BIRTHPLACE: Gainesville, Florida

HEIGHT: 5'4"

WEIGHT: 115 lbs.

HAIR: Brown

EYES: Brown

FAMILY: Dad, Sergio, Sr.; mom, Genoveda Ojeda. Sergio is an only child.

LANGUAGES SPOKEN: Spanish, English and Portuguese

JOINED MENUDO: January 27, 1986, replacing Roy Rossello

FAVORITE COLOR: Blue

FAVORITE SPORTS: Swimming, running

FAVORITE MOVIES: *Star Wars*, *Tootsie*

FAVORITE FOOD: Lasagna

FAVORITE PASTIMES: Traveling and playing video games

FAVORITE VIDEO GAME: TRON

FAVORITE ACTOR: Sylvester Stallone

FAVORITE HOBBIES: Music, dance and drama

FIRST PROFESSIONAL JOB: Acting in a television commercial in Puerto Rico

INSTRUMENT PLAYED: Synthesizer

DEBUT MENUDO PERFORMANCE: Caracas, Venezuela

BIGGEST INFLUENCE ON HIS LIFE: His parents

IDEAL GIRL: Sergio likes someone intelligent and fun to be with

WHERE TO WRITE TO SERGIO: Sergio Gonzales
Menudo
c/o Padosa Av.
Ponce de Leon 157
Hato Rey, Puerto Rico 00913

RICKY MARTIN

"It was always my dream to be a member of Menudo," smiles Ricky Martin, who joined the group in July, 1984. He was born Enrique Martin Morales on December 24, 1971 in Hato Rey, Puerto Rico and grew up in a large family which includes three brothers and one sister.

He has always been very close to his family and found it very difficult to be separated from them when he first joined Menudo. "I think being away made me grow up a little more," he says. "Because out of the whole year, I'm with my family only four months and I had to learn a lot of responsibilities." To cure his homesick blues, brown-eyed Ricky wrote letters to his family and friends.

Traveling all over the world on tour has been a highlight for this fan of Van Halen and Michael Jackson. "I've learned a lot through my travels with the group," he says. He loves learning about history and making friends in countries like Japan and the Philippines. One of Ricky's hobbies is collecting keychains from everywhere Menudo plays and he's built up a very nice collection over the years.

When Ricky isn't working on new dance steps or recording with the group, he likes going home and spending time with his family. He enjoys swimming and playing sports with his friends in Puerto Rico. "It's been easy for me," he says. "All my friends are just normal guys like me and no one has ever treated me different because I'm in the group."

Next year, Ricky will probably be replaced and after being a Menudo member for almost four years, he says the thing he will miss most are the fans. In fact, he confesses that most of his energy comes from the fans. Ricky isn't sure what he wants to do after Menudo, but one of his dreams is to become a pilot. Whatever he decides, this ambitious guy is bound to be the best at everything he attempts.

RICKY MARTIN'S VITAL STATISTICS

FULL REAL NAME: Enrique Martin Morales

NICKNAMES: Kiki, Little Ricky

BIRTHDATE: December 24, 1971

BIRTHPLACE: Hato Rey, Puerto Rico

HEIGHT: 5'5"

WEIGHT: 130 lbs.

HAIR: Brown

EYES: Brown

FAMILY: Dad, Enrique, Sr.; mom, Merelda; brothers and sisters, Fernando, Angel, Eric and Vanessa

BEST FRIEND: Ex-Menudo Ricky Melendez

JOINED MENUDO: July 1984

FAVORITE SPORTS: Soccer, volleyball, horseback riding, swimming

FAVORITE MUSICIANS: Van Halen, Michael Jackson

FAVORITE PASTIME: "I love traveling and seeing other countries!"

RECORDING DEBUT: Menudo LP *Evolucion*

BIGGEST INFLUENCE ON HIS LIFE: His parents

IDEAL GIRL: "I like girls who are serious and responsible!"

FAVORITE HOBBY: Ricky collects keychains from everywhere he visits

LITTLE-KNOWN FACT: Ricky is left-handed

SECRET DREAM: To become a pilot

SELF-DESCRIPTION: "I'm serious most of the time," he says. "I like to eat and sleep a lot, too."

FAVORITE FUN SPOT: Hawaii

WHERE TO WRITE TO RICKY: Ricky Martin
Menudo
c/o Padosa Av.
Ponce de Leon 157
Hato Rey, Puerto Rico 00913

RALPHY RODRIGUEZ

Ever since sweet Ralphy Rodriguez was ten years old, he dreamed of becoming a member of Menudo. The ambitious dark-brown-haired doll took dancing and singing lessons and waited for the next Menudo to be replaced so he would have a chance.

In late December 1986, Charlie Rivera was about to bid the group farewell and Menudo started auditioning boys to take his place. Out of the three hundred boys who tried out, Ralphy was the lucky one chosen. When he heard the news, he says his first thought was of all the countries he wanted to visit. "I knew as a Menudo member I was going to get the chance to travel around the world and I was real excited about it," he says.

His dream came true because Ralphy's first concert with Menudo was in the Philippines. "I was a little nervous in the beginning," he admits. "The first concert, I was just standing on the stage tapping my foot. It wouldn't stop tapping," he giggles, thinking back.

The next thing Ralphy did with the group was appear in a soap opera in Argentina. "The fans followed us everywhere we went," he says. "I really love meeting all our fans and signing autographs."

Ralphy also loves going to the movies and shopping. "I shop for clothes and electronic games the most," he asserts. "The first thing I bought when I joined Menudo was a tennis racquet because I left mine at home."

When Ralphy isn't recording or touring with the group, he can most likely be found doing his schoolwork, drawing or horseback riding. The Menudo guys all get along well and Ralphy smiles, "Now that I've been with the group for a little while, it's more or less everything I thought it would be — fun!"

RALPHY RODRIGUEZ'S VITAL STATISTICS

FULL REAL NAME: Ralph Rodriguez

BIRTHDATE: April 17; 1974

BIRTHPLACE: Rio Piedras, Puerto Rico

HEIGHT: 5'3"

WEIGHT: 103 lbs.

HAIR: Dark brown

EYES: Dark brown

FAMILY: Dad, Rafael; mom, Miriam; brother, Jose Eduardo

JOINED MENUDO: January 1, 1987, replacing Charlie Rivera

LANGUAGES SPOKEN: Spanish, English

FAVORITE SCHOOL SUBJECTS: Math, Science, English

FAVORITE SINGER: Madonna

FAVORITE FOOD: Chinese, Italian

FAVORITE SPORT: Horseback riding

FAVORITE HOBBY: Drawing

FAVORITE PASTIMES: Going to the movies and going shopping

TYPICAL DAY FOR RALPHY: "We're in the studio all day long," he says. "Sometimes ten o'clock to eight o'clock."

GIRLFRIEND: "I used to have a girlfriend. Just before they picked me for Menudo, she left me for another guy!"

IDEAL GIRL: Her looks aren't as important to Ralphy as a nice personality.

SELF-DESCRIPTION: "I like to joke around a lot, but I can be serious, too."

WHERE TO WRITE TO RALPHY: Ralphy Rodriguez
Menudo
c/o Padosa Av.
Ponce de Leon 157
Hato Rey, Puerto Rico 00913

GEORGE MICHAEL

George Michael was seven years old when he decided to become a musician. He spent most of his youth pursuing that dream. Born to Jack and Leslie Panayiotu on June 25, 1963 in Finchley, North London, his family moved to Warrford when George was twelve.

At his new school, he was placed under the guidance of Andrew Ridgeley and the two boys immediately became friends. When they graduated, George and Andrew formed a band, The Executives. Unfortunately, nothing came of it and George found himself working as a movie theatre usher, a stockroom boy and a disc jockey.

Finally, in 1981, George and Andrew formed Wham! and recorded a demo tape of three of their songs. Their careers immediately took off when they were signed to a record deal and recorded their first single, *Wham! Rap*. By early 1983, Wham! hits were finding their way to America and Columbia Records signed them to a contract.

Their first album, *Fantastic*, sold well, but their second, *Make It Big*, was a giant hit for them. The single *Wake Me Up Before You Go-Go* climbed the charts and earned George and Andrew a Grammy nomination for Best Pop Performance by a Duo. Their world tour was a success and they made history as the first Western group to perform in communist China.

Then in 1986, George and Andrew went their separate ways and George set out on his own. His first solo single, *I Want Your Sex*, is breaking new barriers in music and climbing the charts as well. Of Wham!'s breakup, George says, "We just decided to call it quits and we split up with no hard feelings."

George Michael has proven that ambition, talent and good looks mix well. Because he definitely has all three!

GEORGE MICHAEL'S VITAL STATISTICS

FULL REAL NAME: Georgios Kyriacou Panayiotu

NICKNAME: Yog

BIRTHDATE: June 25, 1963

BIRTHPLACE: Finchley, North London

HEIGHT: 6′

WEIGHT: 160 lbs.

HAIR: Brown

EYES: Brown

FAMILY: Dad, Jack; mom, Leslie; sisters, Yioda, Melanie

EARLY JOBS: DJ, movie usher

FIRST BREAK: Forming Wham! with Andrew Ridgeley and getting a record deal in 1981

FAVORITE COLORS: Brown, blue

FAVORITE BAND: Frankie Goes to Hollywood

FAVORITE SINGER: Elton John

FAVORITE SNACK: Potato chips with mayonnaise

FAVORITE SPORT: Badminton

PASTIMES: Dancing, dining, music

LITTLE KNOWN FACT: He is partially color blind and wears contact lenses.

WHY WHAM! SPLIT UP: "We had taken Wham! as far as it could go and decided to call it quits. We split up with no hard feelings."

HE IS MOST CONFIDENT ABOUT: His songwriting

IDEAL GIRL: Someone bright with a great sense of humor

FUTURE GOALS: Wait and see

WHERE TO WRITE TO GEORGE: George Michael
c/o Columbia Records
51 West 52nd Street
New York, NY 10019

JARED CHANDLER

Jared Chandler had dreams of becoming an actor since age seven. He was born in Belgium and lived in Germany for eight years before his family moved to California.

While attending Vista High School in North San Diego County, Jared performed in numerous high school plays including *Grease*, *Bye Bye Birdie* and *Hayfever*. His sister, Carol, always encouraged him. "My sister got me involved in community theatre," he says. "And I performed in school plays all through junior and senior high."

Green-eyed Jared was also a member of four bands, but says the best experience he had was playing with a rockabilly band called The Jail Boys. "The first band I was with in high school played hardcore punk," recalls Jared. "The second played reggae. The Jail Boys played rockabilly and they were the most successful. It is my favorite music."

After graduation, he moved to Hollywood to pursue a career in acting and won roles in two feature films, *Woo-Woo Kid* and *Blood Diner*. The producers of *The New Monkees* spotted Jared at the ABC sitcom workshop where he was studying. They liked his work and called him for an interview and a screen test.

"When I found out I was cast as a Monkee, I literally jumped up and down," enthuses Jared. "I was very excited!"

In his spare time, this 6′ tall guy is devoted to surfing and rides on a team for Snap Surfboards in Carlsbad, California.

JARED CHANDLER'S VITAL STATISTICS

FULL REAL NAME: Jared Chandler

BIRTHDATE: July 9, 1967

BIRTHPLACE: Belgium

HEIGHT: 6′

WEIGHT: 160 lbs.

HAIR: Brown

EYES: Green

FAMILY: Dad, Milton; mom, Juliet; sister, Carol; brother, Jerry

CURRENT RESIDENCE: Hollywood, California

FIRST ACTING BREAK: He was in high school productions of *Grease*, *Bye Bye Birdie*, *Deadly Crisis* and *Hay Fever*

INSTRUMENT PLAYED: Guitar

PREVIOUS BAND: A rockabilly band called The Jail Boys

MOVIES: *Woo-Woo Kid*, *Bloody Diner*

FAVORITE SPORT: Surfing

FAVORITE ACTORS: James Dean, Jimmy Stewart, Aidan Quinn

FAVORITE MUSIC: Rockabilly

FAVORITE SINGERS: Buddy Holly, Elvis, Chuck Berry, Little Richard, Brian Setzer

IDEAL GIRL: Someone with great eyes, honesty, humor — a quiet sort of girl.

WHERE TO WRITE TO JARED: Jared Chandler
The New Monkees
c/o Columbia Pictures
Television
Columbia Plaza South
Burbank, CA 91505

DINO KOVAS

Dino Kovas' car was hit twice in six days, but he didn't realize how that was going to help him. He decided to save the $1,100 he collected for repairs and put it in the bank. A few days later, the money came in handy. When he read about an open call for four New Monkees, Dino took the money and bought a round trip ticket to New York.

Born in Martins Ferry, Ohio and raised in Dearborn, Michigan, Dino thought it was a dream come true when he was chosen as the drummer of *The New Monkees*. He admits he wanted to play drums as far back as grammar school.

"I remember when I was in the fifth grade, I joined a sixth grade band," says Dino. "I would play the wood blocks and the bells. I guess that is how I eventually got involved with the drums." When he was in eighth grade, he got a little money together and bought an inexpensive drum set.

At seventeen, Dino caught the attention of talent scouts from the *Back Porch Video* television show and was cast as a regular. Then he joined the band Snake Out, which he recently left to begin working as a New Monkee.

Dino found out he'd been cast while in a shopping mall. "I couldn't drive my car because it was wrecked," recalls Dino. "I called my mom to come pick up me and my friend and she told me to call Steve Blauner, the executive producer of *The New Monkees*. I called him from the pay phone at the shopping mall, and when he told me I was cast, I literally dropped the phone and immediately began pounding on my poor friend, Lorenzo."

Dino plans to stay in show business for a long time and says someday he would like to get involved in cinematography and directing.

DINO KOVAS' VITAL STATISTICS

FULL REAL NAME: Dino Kovas
BIRTHDATE: July 1, 1966
BIRTHPLACE: Martins Ferry, Ohio
HEIGHT: 5′9″
WEIGHT: 165 lbs.
HAIR: Brown
EYES: Hazel
FAMILY: His parents divorced when Dino was four years old. He has one sister, Tina

CURRENT RESIDENCE: Dearborn, Michigan
FIRST AMBITION: To be a baseball player
INSTRUMENT PLAYED: Drums
TELEVISION: He was a regular on the show *Back Porch Video*
FIRST BAND: Snake Out
FAVORITE SPORTS: Football, basketball, swimming, track, baseball
IDEAL GIRL: An outgoing girl with a great personality
SELF-DESCRIPTION: "I have always felt my personality was a cross between Micky Dolenz and Lou Costello of Abbott and Costello," he says.
FUTURE GOALS: Eventually Dino would like to get involved in cinematography and directing
HIS AUDITION FOR *THE NEW MONKEES:* "They asked me to sing a song for them. 'What could you come up with,' they asked me. I said, 'probably an old Elvis tune,' and I think they liked the fact that I didn't say I'd sing *I'm A Believer*."
WHERE TO WRITE TO DINO: Dino Kovas
                                              The New Monkees
                                              c/o Columbia Pictures
                                                   Television
                                              Columbia Plaza South
                                              Burbank, CA 91505

MARTY ROSS

The oldest New Monkee, Marty Ross, grew up in a musical household. Having played classical guitar and violin since the age of five, Marty knew right from the beginning that he wanted to pursue a career in music.

"My mother, Margaret, was a folk guitarist," says Marty, who was born in Eugene, Oregon. "I remember when she played in front of a group of people, everyone would be very still and in total awe of her. I have always liked being the center of attention and through music, I knew I could be."

Marty was part of a band called The Wigs, which wrote eight songs for the film *My Chauffeur*. The producers of *The New Monkees* saw the band and asked them to audition for the series. "I knew there was no way I would be chosen for the part of a Monkee," admits blue-eyed Marty. "I was twenty-seven years old and I knew the talent scouts were looking for guys between the ages of eighteen and twenty-one."

One of 5,000 applicants, Marty was selected after seven auditions and two screen tests. "I feel real thankful for the opportunity," he says. "In fact, I almost quit the business to get into something that offered more security. Now I can call my mom and tell her I got a job!"

When Marty has some time off, he enjoys collecting baseball cards and records of the 60s, playing table tennis and reading. And now this Los Angeles, California resident looks forward to collecting old cars, too!

MARTY ROSS' VITAL STATISTICS

FULL REAL NAME: Martin Ross
BIRTHDATE: June 5, 1959
BIRTHPLACE: Eugene, Oregon
HEIGHT: 6'2"
WEIGHT: 180 lbs.
HAIR: Brown
EYES: Blue
FAMILY: Dad, Professor Gordon Ross; mom, Margaret

FIRST GUITAR: "My mom was a folk singer and I took it from her. It was a ukulele, smaller than a guitar, and it only had four strings, but I learned everything I know from it," he says.

FIRST BAND: The Wigs

INSTRUMENT PLAYED: Bass

FAVORITE PASTIME: Collecting baseball cards and records from the 60s

FAVORITE SPORT: Table tennis

FAVORITE MUSICIANS: "XTC. I think they are the best group. They're from England."

CURRENT RESIDENCE: Los Angeles, California

IDEAL GIRL: Honest, sincere, someone who can talk out her problems — especially with him!

SELF-DESCRIPTION: "I think I represent maturity and have a license to be crazy when I want to."

WHERE TO WRITE TO MARTY: Marty Ross
The New Monkees
c/o Columbia Pictures
  Television
Columbia Plaza South
Burbank, CA 91505

LARRY SALTIS

Blond-haired Larry Saltis was in his third week of school at Kent State University in Ohio when he received a call telling him he was one of the nine finalists selected for *The New Monkees*. Excited over the news, Larry packed his bags, went to Hollywood for a screen test and at 18, was selected as the youngest member of the group.

"I remember waiting in line for four hours and being interviewed for thirty seconds," says Larry with a smile. "I was very excited and surprised when I heard I was cast. I really felt I was in the right place at the right time."

Larry, who was born in Columbus, Ohio, has been playing the guitar since age seven, and at first he had no intentions of becoming an actor. In fact, it was his parents, Gail and Lawrence, who saw the advertisement on MTV for open auditions for *The New Monkees* and surprised their talented son with two tickets to New York for the auditions.

Larry says he was told one of the reasons he was chosen was because of his winning smile. Comparing the new show to the original Monkees TV series, Larry comments, "I think we have the same kind of stories and slap-stick comedy. But there's more music and video."

This fan of Billy Idol would eventually like to finish college. For the moment, though, he's concentrating on life as a New Monkee.

LARRY SALTIS' VITAL STATISTICS

FULL REAL NAME: Lawrence Saltis

BIRTHDATE: March 25, 1968

BIRTHPLACE: Columbus, Ohio

HEIGHT: 5'11"

WEIGHT: 165 lbs.

HAIR: Sandy blond

EYES: Brown

FAMILY: Parents, Gail and Dr. Lawrence Saltis; brother, Heath

PETS: Dog, Kenny, and cat, Scottie

CURRENT RESIDENCE: Akron, Ohio

LITTLE KNOWN FACT: Larry is the youngest New Monkee

INSTRUMENT PLAYED: Guitar

IDEAL GIRL: "She has to understand that I am a normal person and she has to enjoy music and entertainment," he says.

FAVORITE SPORTS: Karate, soccer

FAVORITE PASTIME: Teaching guitar

FAVORITE SINGER: Billy Idol

FUTURE GOALS: "My main interest is music, but I will continue my studies at college through correspondence courses."

WHERE TO WRITE TO LARRY: Larry Saltis
The New Monkees
c/o Columbia Pictures
   Television
Columbia Plaza South
Burbank, CA 91505

JACK WAGNER

It seems everything Jack Wagner attempts turns to gold. As a young boy growing up in Washington, Missouri, he took up golf and at the age of twelve was regularly winning golf matches. During high school, he continued to play, but also began appearing in school plays.

Despite winning the Missouri State Junior College Golf Championship, Jack remained undecided about which career to concentrate on after high school. He first attended Missouri University, but couldn't get acting out of his system and transferred to East Central College where he was the star of almost every campus production. He was given an acting scholarship and transferred to the University of Arizona, from which he graduated in 1982.

After college, Jack moved to Los Angeles and held many jobs while auditioning for roles in TV shows. He won small parts in the soaps *A New Day in Eden* and *Knots Landing* and was "discovered" by the *General Hospital* producers when they saw him in the play *The Boar Hug*. "I was hired strictly on acting ability," insists Jack. "It was later that they heard me sing."

His first two albums, *All I Need* and *Lighting Up The Night,* were smash hits and Jack's role on *General Hospital* continued to expand. It seemed like he was finally settled happily into two careers, but when his third LP, *Don't Give Up Your Day Job*, was released in early 1987, Jack decided to give up his day job on *General Hospital*.

He toured in a road production of *West Side Story* during the summer of 1987, when his dream of appearing on stage came true again. Looking ahead to his future, he wants to continue acting, and his goal is to do a Broadway show. "I don't see why a person can't do more than just one thing well," he says. "I want to explore everything!"

JACK WAGNER'S VITAL STATISTICS

FULL REAL NAME: Peter John Wagner, Jr.

NICKNAME: "J"

BIRTHDATE: October 3, 1959

BIRTHPLACE: Washington, Missouri

HEIGHT: 5'11"

WEIGHT: 165 lbs.

HAIR: Sandy brown

EYES: Hazel

FAMILY: Dad, Peter, Sr., mom, Irene (but everyone calls her "Scottie"); brothers, Dennis and Jerry; half sister, Joan

CAR: Blue Ford Bronco

FAVORITE SPORT: Golf

FAVORITE FOOD: Oriental

FAVORITE FILMS: *The Goodbye Girl, The Godfather*

FAVORITE ACTRESS: Katharine Hepburn

FAVORITE ACTOR: Jack Nicholson

FAVORITE MUSICIANS: Phil Collins, Van Halen, Neil Young

FAVORITE DESSERT: Pecan pie

FIRST JOBS: Tour guide for Universal Studios, doorman at a bar, waiter, clothing store salesman

FIRST SOAP OPERA ROLE: Clint Masterson in *New Day in Eden*

TELEVISION: Guest appearance on *Knots Landing, General Hospital*

ALBUMS: *All I Need* (EP and LP), *Lighting up the Night, Don't Give Up Your Day Job*

IDEAL GIRL: Someone independent, ambitious and sincere

SECRET FANTASY: To go skydiving

FUTURE GOAL: To do a Broadway show

WHERE TO WRITE TO JACK: Jack Wagner
P.O. Box 1608
St. Louis, MO 63188

PAUL YOUNG

Paul Young is a fast-rising superstar who catapulted his way to the top of the U.S. charts with hits like *Everytime You Go Away* and *Everything Must Change*. His good looks and irresistible smile have placed him not only at the top of the charts, but also in the hearts of his enthusiastic fans. A fan of sixties soul himself, Paul says he feels he's finally doing the kind of music he really enjoys.

He was born Paul Anthony Young on January 17, 1956 and grew up in the English town of Luton in Belfordshire. At the age of fourteen, he was encouraged by his father to take piano lessons and discovered his love for music.

Having mastered the guitar as well as the piano, Paul joined his first serious band, Streetband, in 1978. Unfortunately, after the success of one novelty tune, *Toast*, the band broke up in 1979.

Paul and fellow members John Gifford and Mick Pearl formed the Q-Tips, which Paul loved being part of. They played soul — the music they enjoyed — and the Q-Tips became one of the most popular and exciting bands on stage. In 1982, however, they disbanded because of poor record sales.

That same year, CBS records signed Paul as a solo artist. He quickly caught on as "the best white soul singer Britain ever produced" and in 1983, he toured the United States. He was hoping to achieve the same popularity in America as he had in England, but still wasn't prepared for the enthusiasm American fans had for him. He reached star status in only a short time and his record *Everytime You Go Away* soared on the charts.

This handsome Brit rocker married Stacy Smith in Tahoe, and the couple recently had a daughter, Levi. As for his music, Paul hopes to maintain his popularity and continue to "make money, stay happy and sing!"

PAUL YOUNG'S VITAL STATISTICS

FULL REAL NAME: Paul Anthony Young

NICKNAME: Royal

BIRTHDATE: January 17, 1956

BIRTHPLACE: Luton, Bedfordshire, England

HEIGHT: 6'1"

WEIGHT: 165 lbs.

HAIR: Brown

EYES: Blue

FAMILY: Dad, Tony; mom, Doris; one older brother and one younger sister

FIRST RECORD HE EVER BOUGHT: *Riders On The Storm* by The Doors

FAVORITE SINGERS: Otis Redding, Marvin Gaye, Smokey Robinson

FAVORITE GROUP: The Doors

FAVORITE FOOD: Indian

FAVORITE DRINK: Tequilla and orange

THE MOST ROMANTIC THING YOU EVER DID: "Serenade a girl on her birthday wearing a sombrero and playing a guitar."

THE MOST ROMANTIC THING YOU HAD DONE TO YOU: "A girl sent me a single rose every day for one month."

PERSONAL AMBITION: "Stay as happy as I am right now!"

PROFESSIONAL AMBITION: "Make money, stay happy and sing!"

BEST EXPERIENCE AS A SINGER: "Probably when I played for Prince Charles and Princess Diana at the Royal Albert Hall charity concert for the Prince's Trust."

WORST EXPERIENCE AS A SINGER: "When my band the Q-Tips broke up."

WHERE TO WRITE TO PAUL: Paul Young
c/o Columbia Records
51 West 52nd Street
New York, NY 10019

DWEEZIL ZAPPA

Dweezil Zappa's first album, *Havin' A Bad Day*, was a family effort. His dad, veteran rock musician Frank Zappa, produced it; his sister, Moon Unit, sang on two tracks, and it was recorded in the family's home studio, Utility Muffin Research Kitchen.

Handsome Dweezil was born on September 5, 1969 and lives in Southern California with his family. That includes mom, Gail, another sister, Diva, and brother Ahmet. Dweezil's description of life at home is "happy, bizarre, exciting and amusing."

An accomplished guitarist, he began playing the instrument at a very young age and at thirteen, released his first single, *My Mother is a Space Cadet*. Since then, he's built up his reputation by playing on his father's albums as well as Don Johnson's *Heartbeat* LP. In 1986, he also began his twelve-week-a-year stint as MTV's permanent fill-in DJ.

Green-eyed Dweezil expanded his talents onto the silver screen when he landed a small role in *National Lampoon's European Vacation*. He followed that with *Pretty in Pink* and Dweezil's latest film is the futuristic adventure *The Running Man*. This talented guy, however, is undecided about whether he wants to continue acting or go back to music.

Looking ahead, he says, "Mainly I just want to make a living from something I enjoy." However, he does have his heart set on two things he'd like to accomplish in the near future. "Well, I love the music of Madonna," he begins. "So one would be to play on her next record. And the other is to buy a house in Hawaii." There's no doubt Dweezil's future dreams will come true, just as they have in the past.

DWEEZIL ZAPPA'S VITAL STATISTICS

FULL REAL NAME: Dweezil Zappa
BIRTHDATE: September 5, 1969
BIRTHPLACE: Los Angeles, California
HEIGHT: 5'9½"
WEIGHT: 140 lbs.
HAIR: Brown
EYES: Green
FAMILY: Dad, Frank; mom, Gail; brother, Ahmet Emuuka Rodan; sisters, Diva and Moon Unit

PET: Cats, Gorgo, Marshmoff, Tweezer, Mario, Nekko and dogs, Max and Dogess

Car: Black BMW

FAVORITE GUITARISTS: Eddie Van Halen, Warren DiMartini from Ratt

FAVORITE MUSICIANS: Madonna, Ratt, Van Halen, Frank Zappa

FAVORITE ACTRESS: Mia Sara

FAVORITE COMEDIAN: Bob Goldthwaite

FAVORITE FOOD: Italian

FAVORITE SPORTS: Baseball, basketball

FAVORITE VACATION SPOT: Hawaii

HOBBIES: Playing guitar — and sleeping!

ALBUM: *Havin' A Bad Day*

MOVIES: *National Lampoon's European Vacation*, *Pretty in Pink*, *The Running Man*

FUTURE GOALS: "I want to play on Madonna's next record and work with Mia Sara."

WHERE TO WRITE TO DWEEZIL: Dweezil Zappa
P.O. Box 5265
North Hollywood, CA 91616

ABOUT THE AUTHOR

Grace Catalano is the editor of the popular teen magazine *Dream Guys* and the author of *Kirk Cameron: Dream Guy* (Bantam). She has interviewed scores of celebrities and her articles have appeared in numerous magazines. She and her brother, Joseph, wrote and designed *Elvis — A 10th Anniversary Tribute*. Grace lives with her family in Valley Stream, New York.

FREE!!
BOOKS BY MAIL
CATALOGUE

BOOKS BY MAIL will share with you our current bestselling books as well as hard to find specialty titles in areas that will match your interests. You will be updated on what's new in books at no cost to you. Just fill in the coupon below and discover the convenience of having books delivered to your home.

PLEASE ADD $1.00 TO COVER THE COST OF POSTAGE & HANDLING.

- -

BOOKS BY MAIL
320 Steelcase Road E.,
Markham, Ontario L3R 2M1

IN THE U.S. -
210 5th Ave., 7th Floor
New York, N.Y., 10010

Please send Books By Mail catalogue to:

Name _____
(please print)

Address _____

City _____

Prov./State _____ P.C./Zip _____

(BBM1)